Vocabulary Skills for Students & Teachers
Volume 1

Who is this book for?

This book is designed for three groups of students. The first group is the 7 to 12 year olds, who are working towards Key Stage 2 SATs Assessment Tests in Year 6. If you are in this group, then you are at the end of your Primary School stage, and are about to start Secondary School.

The second group is made up of students who are preparing for 11+ exams for independent and grammar schools. This book provides a comprehensive course in spelling, and vocabulary development at this stage; together with comprehension and word-power development skills, needed for both verbal reasoning and creative writing.

The third group is made up of 7 to 12 year olds, who work independently at home or in school. All of the books in this series are free-standing, so a child can work through each of them or focus on the individual subject needs of the child.

Whichever group you belong to, your confidence and competence will grow, as you practice and improve your knowledge for life with these exercises. As your knowledge of English vocabulary expands, you will be excited and motivated by your developing skills and improved performance, not only in school but in life generally.

About This Book
This book **supports the whole of the Key Stage 2 English curriculum** for success in literacy. It will help you to develop your vocabulary and spelling skills so that you can be successful in learning English. You will not only learn new words and build your vocabulary (word bank) thoroughly, but you will also be motivated to extend your understanding and demonstrate this in both school work and out of school activities.

Other books in this Series are:
- *English Grammar: A Student's Companion*
- *Mastering Comprehension Skills*
- *Spelling & Word-Power Skills*
- *11+ English Preparation Tests for the CEM*
- *Vocabulary Skills for Students & Teachers – Volumes 1 & 2*

How the book is organized
This innovative approach to word-power building has been used by the author in classrooms for over 20 years, among children as young as 7 years. It was noticed that deliberately teaching vocabulary as a subject to students and making linkages to the meaning of the words to situations they already knew, in an animated and fun way, made their experiences rich and alive with excitement. English became for those children, an exciting and fascinating subject that they excelled in; as they tried out their new-found word power in their written and spoken English. As a result, many succeeded in State, Grammar school, 11+ examinations and Independent School selection exams; as well as achievement of Level 5 and above for Year 6 pupils in the annual SATs tests.

You are encouraged to spell the words and learn the list of **600 words** and their definitions in the **60 Units** that are provided. You are then encouraged to test your knowledge in the **gap-filling exercises** which follow each Unit. *Please note you may be required to change the class of the word in the vocabulary gap-filling exercises, so that it makes grammatical sense, e.g. adding ed/ing/es/s, etc.* Additionally, **testing the formation of words in different grammatical word classes,** as well as 60 practical **Vocabulary Development Tests in 16**

© 2018 Roselle Thompson   *Vocabulary Skills Building Workbook – Volume I*

Crossword puzzles; make the whole experience fun, empowering and enjoyable. In addition, helpful **Tips & Challenges** to understand the structure of English are enclosed.

One of the unique aspects of this Book is the fact that it presents **a panorama of the United Kingdom** via **39** stimulating **general knowledge Quiz Challenges** that help to reinforce the idea that your knowledge of English must be holistic or well rounded, so that you enjoy your learning, not in a robotic way but alive to the creative world around you, which has given you the English language.

Many students learn formulaic techniques in a mechanical way, for school entrance tests which, at times, spoil their enjoyment of English language, because they do so just to get through the tests. In fact, experience has shown that many children could do with far more expansion of their personal knowledge of things around them and general information which relate to them, in many other non-school ways. This is one reason why we have put some brain-teasing *"Did you know"* facts to help children expand their horizons and become alive to the general knowledge within the world in which they live, in a really fun way.

DID YOU KNOW? This section of the book, with a variety of **Quiz Challenges**, is designed to sharpen your skills and attitude to learning. They test your general knowledge and are located at the bottom of the vocabulary exercises in this book. They are also designed to help you become more aware of extra knowledge which you should gain to expand your knowledge and vocabulary generally. Try the questions and see how much you know! These very exciting facts are all about the United Kingdom! *(Answers on the back pages)*

A **Certificate of Achievement** is provided at the end of the book to give you a sense of reward for your hard work in completing the book. **Answers for each Vocabulary Test are also provided at the back of the book** to help you mark and evaluate your progress.

The right of Roselle Thompson to be identified as the Author of this work has been asserted by her in accordance with the Copyright, Designs & Patents Act 1988.

All rights reserved including translations. No part of this publication may be reproduced in any material form (including photocopying or storing it in any medium by electronic means and whether or not transiently or incidentally to some other sue of this publication), without the written permission of the copyright owner, except in accordance with the provisions of the Copyright, Designs and Patents Act 1988. Applications for the copyright owner's written permission to reproduce any part of this publication should be addressed to the publisher – **Eagle Publications**.

Warning: The doing of an unauthorized act in relation to this copyright work may result in court action as a claim for damages and criminal prosecution.

Published in the UK by: Eagle Publications, P O Box 73374, London W3 3FZ, UK
Email: eaglepublications58@gmail.com   www.eaglepublications.co.uk
Enquiries: 07739655603 or 07848844377

Crosswords: www.crosswordlabs.com
Cover design: V3 Creative Designs

© **Roselle Thompson**   ISBN **978-0-9542325-2-8**

Phoenix Study Guides

Vocabulary Skills For Students & Teachers:
A Practical Toolkit
Volume 1

By

Roselle Thompson

This book belongs to:

Name..

EAGLE PUBLICATIONS

© 2018 Roselle Thompson   *Vocabulary Skills Building Workbook – Volume I*

CONTENTS PAGE

Understanding English	1	Unit 19 & Unit 19 Test	31	Crossword Puzzle No.11	61
Root words	2	Prefixes	31	Unit 43 & Unit 43 Test	62
Suffixes	3	Unit 20 & Unit 20 Test	32	Synonyms & Antonyms	62
Unit 1 & Unit 1 Test	6	Noun formation	33	Verb formation	63
Homographs	6	Crossword Puzzle No. 5	34	Unit 45 & Unit 45 Test	64
Unit 2 & Unit 2 Test	8	Unit 22 & Unit 22 Test	35	Crossword Puzzle No.12	65
Unit 3 & Unit 3 Test	9	Adjective formation	35	Unit 46 & Unit 46 Test	66
Unit 4 & Unit 4 Test	10	Unit 23 & Unit 23 Test	36	Unit 47 & Unit 47 Test	67
Word building	10	Unit 24 & Unit 24 Test	37	Verb Formation	67
Unit 5 & Unit 5 Test	11	Crossword Puzzle No. 6	38	Unit 48 & Unit 48 Test	68
Crossword Puzzle No.1	12	Unit 25 & Unit 25 Test	39	Unit 49 & Unit 49 Test	69
Unit 5 & Unit 6 Test	13	Unit 26 & Unit 26 Test	40	Synonyms & Antonyms	69
Antonyms	13	Prefixes	40	Crossword Puzzle No.13	70
Synonyms	13	Unit 27 & Unit 27 Test	41	Unit 50 & Unit 50 Test	71
Unit 7 & Unit 7 Test	14	Unit 28 & Unit 28 Test	42	Verb formation	71
Noun formation	14	Crossword Puzzle No. 7	43	Unit 51 & Unit 51 Test	72
Unit 8 & Unit 8 Test	15	Unit 29 & Unit 29 Test	44	Synonyms & Antonyms	72
Noun formation	15	Synonyms & Antonyms	44	Unit 52 & Unit 52 Test	73
Unit 9 & Unit 9 Test	16	Unit 30 & Unit 30 Test	45	Unit 53 & Unit 53 Test	74
Compound Words	16	Unit 31 & Unit 31 Test	46	Synonyms & Antonyms	74
Unit 10 & Unit 10 Test	17	Synonyms	46	Crossword Puzzle No. 14	75
Adjective formation	17	Crossword Puzzle No. 8	47	Unit 54 & Unit 54 Test	76
Unit 11 & Unit 11 Test	18	Unit 32 & Unit 32 Test & Verb formation	48	Describing Personalities	76
Synonyms	18	Unit 33 & Unit 33 Test	49	Unit 55 & Unit 55 Test	77
Crossword Puzzle No. 2	19	Noun Formation	49	Unit 56 & Unit 56 Test	
Unit 12 & Unit 12 Test	20	Unit 34 & Unit 34 Test	50	Quick Test	78
Adjective/Verb/Noun formation	20	Unit 35 & Unit 35 Test	51	Unit 57 & Unit 57 Test	79
Unit 13 & Unit 13 Test	21	Noun formation	51	Verb formation	79
Synonyms & Antonyms	21	Crossword Puzzle No. 9	52	Crossword Puzzle No. 15	
Homophones	22	Unit 36 & Unit 36 Test	53	Unit 58 & Unit 58 Test	81
Verb formation	23	Synonyms & Antonyms	53	Unit 59 & Unit 59 Test	82
Unit 14 & Unit 14 Test	24	Unit 37 & Unit 37 Test	54	Opposites	82
Verb formation	24	Noun formation	54	Unit 60 & Unit 60 Test	83
Crossword Puzzle No. 3	25	Unit 38 & Unit 38 Test	55	Synonyms	83
Unit 15 & Unit 15 Test	26	Crossword Puzzle No. 10	56	Crossword Puzzle No. 16	84
Adjective formation	26	Unit 39 & Unit 39 Test	57	Glossary	85
Unit 16 & Unit 16 Test	27	Adverb formation	57	Unit Tests - *Answers*	90
Noun formation	27	Unit 40 & Unit 40 Test	58	Crossword - *Answers*	104
Unit 17 & Unit 17 Test	28	Verb formation	58	*Do you Know* Challenges pages:1,3,4,5,6,7,9,10,11,13,15,16,20, 23,30,31,32,26,27,39,41,45,46, 49,50,54,55,57,60,64,66,68,73, 76,77,81,82,83 *Answers pg 94*	
Synonyms & Antonyms	28	Unit 41 & Unit 41 Test	59		
Crossword Puzzle No. 4	29	Synonyms & Antonyms	59		
Unit 18 & Unit 18 Test	30	Unit 42 & Unit 42 Test	60		
Suffixes	30	Similar meanings	60		

UNDERSTANDING THE ENGLISH LANGUAGE

Did you know that many words from different languages have found their way into the English language and are being used as common English words?

The English language has borrowed words from many parts of the world. Here are some examples of words used as English words from around the world:

Words	Country/origin	Words	Country/origin
Haiku	Japan	Patio	Spain
Mustang	Spanish	Restaurant	French
Spaghetti	Italy	Macaroni	Italy
Yatch	Dutch	Pyjamas	India
Kayak	Eskimo	Shampoo	India
Frankfurter	Frankfurt, Germany	Jukebox	USA
Admiral	Arabic	Canoe	Caribbean
Dictator	Latin		

Throughout this book, you will be asked to change certain words into classes. This is because you must be aware that English words can be classified into different categories or **Parts of Speech**.

This is because each word plays a part in our speech or when we make sentences. The main categories that English words fall into are:

1. **Nouns** – name words for people, places or things e.g. *John, London, books*
2. **Verbs** – action or doing words e.g. *climb, jump, drive*
3. **Pronouns** – words used instead of using a name word e.g. *he, she, it*
4. **Adjectives** – words that describe nouns or pronouns e.g. *sunny, wet, dark*
5. **Adverbs** – words that tell us the actions of verbs e.g. *fast, heavily, quietly*
6. **Conjunctions** – used for joining clauses or sentences e.g. *and, but, because*
7. **Prepositions** – show the relationship between things e.g. *on, in, over*
8. **Exclamations** – express surprise or sudden emotions e.g. *Stop! Hi! Look!*

Understanding how words function in language, helps your understanding of word-formation, word-building and your ability to use and expand your vocabulary.

Did You Know? *Words that come from the Greek language have* **ph** *or* **f** *in them? Make a list of 10 of your own.*

ROOT WORDS

To get to grips with building vocabulary easily, understanding how words are made up and at times knowing their origin, will help you to work out the meaning of a word. For some words, you will need to look at the beginning part, called **the prefix,** which helps you to understand their meaning.

PREFIXES

Prefixes are the beginning parts of a word that changes their meaning. Some common prefixes are:

im – means *not*
mis – means *not*
pre – means *before*
un – means *not*
il – means *not*
re – means *again*
in – means *not*
under – means *below or less than*

By adding these prefixes to words we can see how their meaning changes:

For example:
*Im*possible
*Mis*trust
*Pre*historic
*Un*happy
*Il*legal
*Re*make
*In*adequate
under*water*

Not all words have prefixes but you will know when a word has a prefix, if the root word is a word by itself. For example, in the word **un-happy**, the **un** means *not*; therefore it's easy to work out that the meaning of the word **unhappy** is **"not happy"**.

Therefore, you will need look at the **root word** or the main part of the word in its simple form. Take for example, the word **quietly**, you will notice that the main part or root word here is **quiet**, but there is also the **ly** which is called the **Suffix**.

SUFFIXES

are parts of words at the end which change their meaning. Here are some of the most common suffixes:

y – means state of or full of
ment – means act of or state of
ness – means quality or state of

ous – means full of
ish - means relating to

Adding **suffixes** to words help you to understand their meaning:
Meat***y***
Nourish***ment***
Happi***ness***
Peril***ous***
blu***ish***

MORE ON SUFFIXES

We add suffixes to words for different reasons:
- ➢ To make adjectives from nouns
- ➢ To make adverbs from adjectives
- ➢ To make nouns from verbs

Suffixes change the spelling of words and this tends to affect mostly the root word. Here are some examples of when changes occur:

1. When a word ends with a ***y*** becomes ***i*** with a suffix.
   For example: beaut***y*** – beautiful
           eas***y***   - eas***ily***
           heav***y*** - heav***ily***

   Exceptions where we keep the ***y*** before the suffix are in words such as:
     copy + ***ing*** = copy***ing***
     reply + ***ing*** = reply***ing***
     dry + ***ing*** = dry***ing***

2. When a word ends with an ***e***, we drop the ***e*** before adding the ***ing***:
     driv***e*** – driv***ing***
     car***e*** – car***ing***
     hop***e*** – hop***ing***
     giv***e*** - giv***ing***

3. When a word has a vowel next to the end letter, we double the end letter to make ***ing*** and some ***ed*** endings:
     chop - chop***ping***
     grab - grab***bing***
     shop - shop***ping***
     swim - swim***ming***
     run   - run***ning***

Challenge: *Where is the Sea Life London Aquarium? South Bank or Bankside?*

4. When there is **a vowel** next to the final *y* we keep the *y* ending and then add the suffix:
    buy – buy***ing***
    pay – pay***ing***
    joy – joy***ful***
    pray – pray***ing***

Try to form words with suffixes with the following:

Add **ed** to the following words:
    reply............................
    pray.............................
    delay ....

Add **able** to the following words:
    pay........................
    justify..........................
    rely.............................

Add **ing** to the following words:
    buy.............................
    try..............................
    obey............................

Add **ous** to the following words:
    luxury.........................
    fury...........................
    vary...........................

Add **er** to the following words:
    heavy.........................
    dirty..........................
    busy........................

Add **ance** to the following words:
    defy..........................
    comply.....................
    vary.........................

Add **al** to the following words:
    betray........................
    deny.........................
    try...........................

Challenge: *Which area in Scotland is known as the remotest part of the British Isles and forms the most important seabird breeding station in north-west Europe?*

MORE ON PREFIXES

There are many words that you can work out the meaning for, with knowledge of how some **prefixes and suffixes** operate within the word. Here are some **uncommon prefixes**:

Prefixes	Meaning	Examples
audio	hear	audible, audience
aqua	water	aquatic, aqueduct
centum	one hundred	century, centenary
clamo	shout	clamour, proclaim, exclaim
creo	create	creature, creation
decem	ten	decade, decimal
dico	say	dictation, verdict
duco	lead	production, introduce
finis	finish	final
homo	man	homicide, human,
liber	to free	liberate, liberty
manus	hand	manual, manufacture
navis	a ship	naval, navy, navigate
octo	eight	october, octagon
plus	more	plural
primus	first	primitive, prime
rego	rule	regina, regiment
scribo	write	script, describe
uns	one	unit, union
video	to see	vision, visible
vanus	empty	vanish

Put Prefixes in these words		Put Suffixes in these words	
………cast	………tell	exist………………	remit………………
………national	………capable	simple………………	create………………
………press	………represent	mercy………………	post………………
………port	………logical	moment………………	human………………
………marine	………meditated	interrupt………………	cigar………………
………able	………treat	comfort………………	public………………
………develop	………judge	erupt………………	wait………………

Challenge: *Where can you shop at the same places as The Queen?*

Vocabulary Exercises (Unit 1)

- **remedy** (n): a cure, something that makes you feel better
- **contented** (adj): happy and satisfied
- **purchase** (v): to buy something
- **placid** (adj): quiet and calm
- **omit** (v): to leave out
- **liberate** (v): to set someone or something free
- **approve** (v): to agree with something
- **incentive** (n): something that is offered to encourage a person
- **miscarriage** (n): an outcome/result you gain by using the wrong method
- **allocate** (v): to select something

Vocabulary Practice Test 1

1. Dad said he does not .... of my sleep over at a friend's house.
2. Last week we .... lots of food for my birthday party.
3. The baby is now quite .... having cried for his food.
4. The doctor gave me a ....for my cough.
5. Our teacher gives us merit awards as an .... for working hard.
6. They discovered a ....of justice in her court trial.
7. The man was caught in the lab as he tried to .... the animals from suffering.
8. The local Council will .... a special park for those who love nature to enjoy the scenery.
9. The new boy is quite ...., unlike his noisy classmates.
10. "I .... to put speech marks in my sentences," said the boy.

VERB FORMATION – form very from these nouns

Nouns	Verbs
pleasure	
knowledge	
thought	
choice	
laughter	
injury	
loss	
remembrance	

Challenge: *Did you know? Some words don't have a plural e.g. money*

USING YOUR DICTIONARY

Every student of English must have a dictionary and a thesaurus. They are important tools, together with this book, to build your English vocabulary. As you develop your vocabulary skills, you will notice that many words have more than one meaning. These are called **Homographs.**

Homographs are words that have the same spelling but different meaning. They may also have different pronunciation and different origins.

wind   the wind we feel around us
to turn by tightening e.g. a clock
to coil around something e.g. bandage
to twist and turn or meander e.g. river

ball   a round object used in tennis, football
a formal social dance

yard   3 feet or 36 inches or 0.9144 metres
the space around a house

count   to count numbers
a European title for a nobleman

race   a contest of speed among people
a person's origin or ethnic group

bear   a wild animal
to endure or experience something

stick   to follow or obey
a broken off shoot or branch of a tree
to attach with glue
to stay close to someone
to cling to something

duck   to lower your head suddenly
a water bird
to dip briefly in water

train   to teach or guide someone
a number of railway carriages pulled together
the back part of a wedding dress that trails behind

mine   possession, belonging to me
an explosive device hidden in the ground
a pit where materials are dug e.g. coal, gold, diamonds

incense   enraged, very angry
a stick that gives off fragrance when burnt

Challenge: *Where is the world's greatest museum of art and design in London?*

Vocabulary Practice Exercises (Unit 2)

- **blunder** (n): a mistake
- **spouse** (n): a husband or wife
- **loathe** (v): to hate or to strongly dislike something
- **eloquent** (adj): to be very good at speaking
- **plummet** (v): to fall from a great height
- **excess** (n): over the limit, excess, or too much
- **define** (v): to say what something means
- **rash** (adj): not carefully thought out
- **flounder** (v): to be clumsy in speaking or thinking
- **curtail** (v): to cut short, come to an unexpected end

Vocabulary Practice Test 2

1. Leaders of countries are supposed to be ………………..and persuasive.
2. The climber slipped and …………………… to his death.
3. The traveler was made to pay for his …………… baggage.
4. Little Children often ……………….. creepy crawlies.
5. The Minister praised his …………. for supporting him over the years.
6. In English, it's important to be able to ……………… words.
7. They made a………………… in her work and had to redo it.
8. He made a …………… ……decision when he bought a faulty car
9. His lack of confidence showed when he ……………… in the interview.
10. The meeting was ………………… when the fire alarm went off.

Spelling your vocabulary words is essential
Tips to help you spell:

- Learn tricky words that don't sound the way we write them e.g. technique,
- Use the look, say, cover, write, check to test yourself, especially difficult words
- Remember syllables help you to work out sections of words as you spell
- Don't always rely on the computer spell-checker, you wont's always have one available when you need it
- Some people use Mnemonics (their own inventions) to help them spell words or remember them e.g. the compass directions **Never Eat Shredded Wheat** for **N**orth, **E**ast, **S**outh and **W**est

Vocabulary Practice Exercises (Unit 3)

- **scornful** (adj): the way in which you turn up your nose at someone,
- **regulation** (n): rules or laws
- **motivation** (n): persuasion or encouragement
- **consent** (n): an agreement or approval
- **perish** (v): easy to be damaged, destroyed or die
- **gloat** (v): to boast or laugh at others
- **absurd** (adj): being ridiculous, utterly senseless or illogical
- **deceive** (v): to trick or fool someone
- **bedlam** (n): confusion and disorder
- **pompous** (adj): being arrogant and conceited

Vocabulary Practice Test 3

1. Dad gave his .... for me to go on a school trip.
2. It is .... to say that you and Prince William are brothers!
3. Although he tried to give me the wrong change, I was not easily ....; I corrected his mistake.
4. We all have to obey the ....of our country.
5. His school report said that because the lacks ...., he does not finish his work.
6. It is not very nice to .... at other people's failings.
7. After five days, the bread and milk .... so we threw them out.
8. The children in class were .... of the new boy with long hair.
9. Rioting and looting on the High Street caused ....
10. He was not shown the way out of the campsite because of his .... attitude towards his friends in the camp.

Did You Know?
All prefixes come from a foreign language. Here are some Anglo-Saxon prefixes: **in, out, for, to, up, over, under, fore, be**. *The main negative prefix is* **un**. *How many words of your own, can you list with these prefixes?*

Vocabulary Practice Exercises (Unit 4)

- **refrain** (v): to stop what you are doing
- **indolent** (adj): very lazy
- **deviate** (v): to change to another route, go another way
- **diligent** (adj): very hard working
- **drab** (adj): untidy-looking
- **misgivings** (n): doubts or concerns
- **refurbish** (v): to redecorate, make changes to a building
- **flamboyant** (adj): being flashy
- **gregarious** (adj): to be sociable or fond of company
- **fickle** (adj): not constant, changeable

Vocabulary Practice Test 4

1. The .... boy was given a detention for not doing his homework.
2. Some children are very .... ; they do all their work and more!
3. The builders are going to .... our home next summer.
4. I have .... about Sally, she is cannot be trusted.
5. The teacher shouted, "Please .... from chatting in my class!"
6. The road was blocked so I had to .... to another route.
7. The tramp looks .... thin and starving.
8. We watched those jolly ladies in their .... hats at the Derby.
9. "Andrew is too .... to be leader of our scouts group," said Sam.
10. The young ballet dancers were quite .... during the competition.

WORD-BUILDING
Form **Adverbs** from these words:

loud	....
peace	....
heavy	....
Comfort	....
Sweet	....
happy	....

Challenge: *What Am I? Since 1753 I have held two million years of human history in my home. You are always invited to come and see.*

Vocabulary Practice Exercise (Unit 5)

- **replica** (n): an exact copy of something
- **intention** (n): an aim or plan or target
- **conditional** (adj): based on a condition, set by someone
- **oppression** (n): the condition that people are in when they are held back people in a country or community
- **reservation** (n): a booking made in advance of an event
- **influential** (adj): having the power to lead and others follow
- **resolution** (n): an agreement with conditions in it
- **yield** (v): to surrender, give way to another
- **ostracise** (v): to isolate, exclude or banish from society
- **distort** (v): to change or alter the true meaning

Vocabulary Practice Test 5

1. It is my ………………… to do well in my 11+ exam.

2. The police will shoot you if you point a ………………… gun at them.

3. Mum made a ………………… at McDonald's restaurant, so we could celebrate by birthday there.

4. Good leaders are ………………… people.

5. We made a ………………… to support all the starving children in developing countries.

6. Some people suffer ………………… in their countries because of bad leadership.

7. The newspaper editor admitted that his paper ………………… the facts.

8. Going to Disney Land is………………… on my passing the 11+ exam.

9. The celebrity felt………………… by some of his fans because he spoke openly about his beliefs.

10. Traffic from the side road had to ………………… to those on the main road.

Challenge: *Where is it?*
King Henry VIII was the most famous resident of this place.

Crossword Puzzle No. 1

Across

4. leave something out
5. set someone or something free
7. calm and quiet
9. happy and satisfied

Down

1. buy something
2. good at speaking
3. encourage someone
6. mistake
8. cure
9. give agreement for something

Vocabulary Practice Exercise (Unit 6)

- **social** (adj): relating to society or the general public
- **portray** (v): what something presents, shows or tells us
- **humiliate** (v): to embarrass or hurt someone's feelings in public
- **resident** (n): a person who lives in an address or area
- **bi-lingual** (adj): speaking two languages
- **restrain** (v): to hold back a person from doing something
- **aspire** (v): to aim or to have a goal in mind to do something
- **facetious** (adj): joking especially in an inappropriate manner
- **thrifty** (adj): being careful with managing money
- **renowned** (adj): to be well known or famous

Vocabulary Practice Test 6

1. The bully .... a boy in front of the whole class.
2. The play .... a love scene between Romeo and Juliet.
3. All the... of this street are our friends.
4. Michael Jackson was .... for his Moon Walk dance.
5. My aunty saved lots of money because she is quite ....
6. My family and I are all ....as we speak English and French.
7. Two teachers had to ....the two boys who were fighting.
8. From now on, I am .... to be an A grade student.
9. It is good to have correct .... manners at all times.
10. Comedians can be .... when they make personal jokes about people's race.

Complete this exercise, the first one has been done for you.

Words	Synonyms (*similar*)	Antonyms (*opposites*)
approve	*agree*	*disapprove*
absurd		
liberate		
remedy		
blunder		
plummet		
loathe		

Challenge: *Name the museum in Liverpool opened in 1853, which has collections and displays of life sciences, earth sciences and human cultures around the world?*

Vocabulary Practice Exercises (Unit 7)

- **resemble** (v): to look like someone
- **stimulation** (n): in a state of being active or alive
- **discrete** (adj): being wise or cautious
- **optimistic** (adj): to have a positive view of life
- **pessimistic** (adj): to have a negative view of life, cynical
- **perspective** (n): a point of view
- **binge** (v): to consume in excess
- **notable** (adj): very important, well-known or famous
- **provisional** (adj): temporary; for the time being
- **accustomed** (adj): being used to doing something

Vocabulary Practice Test 7

1. She crept ………………………. out of the room to answer her mobile phone.
2. Having worked hard, he is ……………………….. about passing the exam.
3. "I am ……………… to working hard and getting good results," she said.
4. The boy and his sister……………………….. each other.
5. We made a ………………………. booking for our dinner party at the restaurant.
6. The ……………………….. boy has not done his school homework for three days, and claims there is no point in doing it!
7. Drinking coffee causes ………………….. that make us temporarily alert.
8. She……………….. on chocolates late at night, that's why she is overweight.
9. It is quite…………………………. that men walked on the moon in 1969.
10. From my ………………….., air pollution should be better managed.

NOUN FORMATION Verbs	Nouns
liberate	
omit	
content	
approve	
eloquent	
define	
absurd	
deceive	

Vocabulary Practice Exercises (Unit 8)

- **submission** (n): in a state of giving up or total obedience
- **slumped** (v): to fall heavily
- **notorious** (adj): well-known for something bad
- **installments** (n): regular payments at agreed times
- **aghast** (adj): to be greatly surprised
- **outburst** (n): an explosion of anger
- **impart** (v): to pass on e.g. learning, knowledge
- **derelict** (adj): old and needing repairs e.g. buildings
- **hinder** (v): to block, stop or obstruct
- **infuriate** (v): to cause anger; or make furious

Vocabulary Practice Test 8

1. "I will pay for my goods by………………….each month," she told the shopkeeper.
2. Hitler was a ………………… man, who killed millions of people.
3. After fainting, the girl ……………………. to the ground.
4. He did as she was told in quiet …………………………..
5. He couldn't contain his ………………….. when the children teased him.
6. The Council is going to demolish those …………………. houses.
7. Teachers …………………….. knowledge to their students.
8. "Don't ……………. me, I want to go into the garden," said the boy.
9. The loud music from next door always ……………….. my grandma.
10. I was ……………..when they said that I had won the competition.

NOUN FORMATION Verbs	Nouns
compete	
humble	
permit	
hero	
simple	
weigh	
sorry	
try	
vain	
terrify	

Challenge: *Do you know what's in the House Cavalry Museum?*

Vocabulary Practice Exercise (Unit 9)

- **dismay** (n): alarm, surprise, or sudden fear
- **placate** (v): to offer something in order to please
- **peruse** (v): to check or examine very carefully
- **fatal** (adj): causing death
- **innovation** (n): a creation or invention
- **negligence** (n): failing to care for someone or something
- **multitude** (n): a huge crowd
- **gorge** (v): to eat greedily
- **frayed** (adj): wear away into threads; at breaking point; irritated
- **gaunt** (adj): looking excessively thin; grim

Vocabulary Practice Test 9

1. "Please .... these documents carefully before signing them," said the Estate Agent.
2. I was .... when I heard that my neighbour had won the lottery!
3. She looks very....................... from dieting and worrying about money.
4. Computer technology these days has created some very exciting ....
5. The pop-star performed in front of a ....of people.
6. The newspaper reported the....................... stabbing of a teacher by a 15 year old boy last week.
7. Due to the parents .... their children were taken away from them.
8. He complained that his nerves were ....from overwork and very little sleep.
9. Many religious people .... their gods by offering food and flowers.
10. The tramp .... himself with food, because he hadn't eaten for a few days.

TASK: Form your own *Compound Words* with any of the words below:

E.g: *rail+way = railway*

Post   ball   cup   our   rail   ache   snow   door   milk   heart
Ground   light   foot   cloth   tooth   water   shop   plane   room   board

Challenge: *Which Roman monument took 15,000 men and 6 years to build, stretches 80 miles from the Solway Coast in Cumbria to Wallsend near Newcastle upon Tyne?*

Vocabulary Practice Exercise (Unit 10)

- **collaborate** (v): to do something jointly or with others
- **allegation** (n): a blame or accusation
- **hypocrite** (n): a person who tells others not to do something but secretly does it
- **uncanny** (adj): a strange coincidence
- **inclement** (adj): very bad weather conditions
- **digress** (v): to wander away from the main topic when speaking or writing
- **initial** (adj): happening first
- **pulverize** (v): to smash into a fine power
- **cynical** (adj): sneering at something that is good
- **appease** (v): to please or pacify

Vocabulary Practice Test 10

1. Tom is a ....; we found him smoking after he told us not to.
2. We expect ....weather on Monday due to a predicted storm.
3. Let's all .... to complete this project quickly.
4. The speaker .... to tell us about his childhood.
5. They made an .... against the nurse but it was not true.
6. After the crash, our .... reaction was to help survivors.
7. It was .... that everyone at the party had the same colour car!
8. Some natives believed that human sacrifices would .... their gods.
9. Tom was .... about Sally's ideas for the art competition, so he was surprised when she won!
10. The workers..... .... the excess stones, then threw the powder into a pit.

ADJECTIVE FORMATION

Words	Adjectives
fame	
sharp	
educate	
provision	
custom	
magnet	
pure	
colony	

Vocabulary Practice Exercise (Unit 11)

- **prospectus** (n): a brochure or information booklet
- **stagnant** (adj): not moving e.g. water; (stagnate – verb)
- **fertile** (adj): able to bear offspring or grow and develop e.g. plants
- **dynamic** (adj): energetic or forceful
- **surmount** (v): to overcome, or rise above
- **veneer** (adj): a superficial appearance, not real
- **intercept** (v): to stop or catch in the act
- **impoverish** (adj): to make poor
- **decrepit** (adj): old and worn out by sicknesses
- **apparition** (n): a ghostly figure

Vocabulary Practice Test 11

1. At the interview we were given a .... of the new school.
2. My garden has very ....soil; I have grown lots of tomatoes.
3. After the flood, ... pools of water could be seen everywhere.
4. The drama group gave a .... performance at our assembly.
5. Running a 800metres race is a difficult task for me to........................
6. The .... man was supported by a Nurse who visited him daily.
7. There is a rumour that the old mansion has an .... of its former owner.
8. The police will .... the escaped criminal at the next junction.
9. This table might be wooden but it definitely has a .... top.
10. The starving children are hungry and ....

SYNONYMS AND OPPOSITES

Words	Synonyms (similar)	Antonyms (opposites)
garrulous		
regress		
vacant		
generosity		
pretend		
dismay		
majority		
vacate		
despicable		
demolish		

Crossword Puzzle No.2

Across

3. ridiculous
5. very lazy
7. very hard-working
9. laws or rules
10. redecorate, make changes

Down

1. boast or laugh at others' faults
2. agreement or approval
4. doubts, concerns
6. make a change from a normal route
8. untidy looking

Vocabulary Practice Exercise (Unit 12)

- **excavate** (v): to dig up, as in old ruins
- **corpse** (n): a dead body
- **disclose** (v): to bring out to the open or tell a secret
- **utilize** (v): to use up or spend
- **retrieve** (v): to recover or restore something to a better state
- **whimsical** (adj): odd, unusual, irrational
- **agitate** (v): to stir up public interest for a cause
- **obstinate** (adj): being stubborn or difficult to handle
- **miser** (n): a greedy, stingy person who hoards money for its own sake
- **misconstrue** (v): to misunderstand or misinterpret someone

Vocabulary Practice Test 12

1. He couldn't keep the secret, so he........................... it.
2. She is..........................her time wisely to prepare for the test.
3. Scientist found buried treasure when they .... the tomb.
4. Firemen brought out the ....of a man from the burning building.
5. Tom .... what his teacher told him; then blamed her for his mistakes.
6. Irene is too ....to ask her for advice, she has very odd ideas.
7. That toddler is quite ...., he needs to be closely monitored.
8. The man lived as a ...., but had millions of pounds when he died.
9. The Worker's Union will .... the public for support of their strike action.
10. The computer has a brilliant system that helps you to .... information that you've lost.

Adjective	Verb	Noun
long		
wide		
instructional		
residential		
conducive		
impressive		

Challenge: This place is the birthplace of England's greatest poet and playwright. Where is it?

Vocabulary Practice Exercise (Unit 13)

- **invest** (v): to put money into a business or project
- **imminent** (adj): happening soon
- **perks** (n): extra benefits apart from your payment for work
- **courteous** (adj): to display good manners and etiquette
- **fabricate** (n): to lie or made up a story to cause suffering
- **mar** (v): to spoil or ruin
- **disparaging** (v): to belittle
- **infatuated** (adj): to have intense but short-lived passion for someone
- **gallant** (adj): very brave
- **intensify** (v): to make or become stronger, or more concentrated

Vocabulary Practice Test 13

1. My dad .... a large sum of money into his friends business.
2. It is very important to be .... to everyone.
3. The bully made some .... remarks about the new pupil.
4. The company offered its staff .... to encourage them to stay.
5. We need to .... our studies, as the exam date is getting closer.
6. Christmas is ....; being only 6 weeks away.
7. She .... lies against her friend, just to be spiteful.
8. The heavy downpour .... our summer's day picnic.
9. The .... knight charged towards his opponent with his sword.
10. Sixteen year old Sally is .... with the sixteen year old boy next door.

SYNONYMS AND OPPOSITES

Words	Synonyms (similar)	Antonyms (opposite)
dispersal		
apprehend		
recuperate		
stationary		
courtesy		
seldom		
contract		
sorrow		
dwarf		
audible		

HOMOPHONES – SAME SOUND/DIFFERENT MEANING

A **Homophone** is a word which has the same sound as another but with a different meaning. It's important to know the differences in their meaning. Here are some very common Homophones. **Learn them and then do the exercise below**.

air	great	night
ate	grate	knight
ball	hear	principal
bawl	heir	principle
beech	heard	reign
beach	herd	rain
boy	here	rein
buoy	heir	right
cellar	hole	write
seller	whole	scent
cereal	him	sent
serial	hymn	stair
check	hour	stare
cheque	our	steal
currant	knot	steel
current	not	stationary
die	leak	stationery
dye	leek	style
ewe	licence	stile
you	license	thrown
ate	lightning	throne
eight	lightening	their
fair	made	there
fare	maid	waist
feat	main	waste
feet	mane	wait
foul	meat	weight
fowl	meet	

Put the correct homophone in the space.

HOMOPHONES TEST

(whole/hole)	The ………………………school went on a school trip.
(weight/wait)	"You must………………until it's your turn," said dad.
(cheque/check)	I will write you a ………………………for £10 pounds.
(cereal/serial)	I have …………………………for my breakfast each day.
(fowl/foul)	The player used …………………language during the game.
(die/dye)	We are going to ……………the material then put it to dry.
(knight/night)	The king's ………………………… was a brave warrior.
(fare/fair)	Have your …………………ready before going on the bus.
(ewe/you)	The farmer's…………………….has given birth to a lamb.
(cellar/seller)	We put our wine in the ……………………….. of our shop.
(Principal/principle)	The ………………… of our college is Mr. Peter Barnes.
(lightning/lightening)	The electricity went out when …………………struck.
(stair/stare)	"Don't just stand there and ………… say hello," said mum.
(main/mane)	We stroke the horse's …………… on our visit to the stable.
(beech/beach)	There is a huge ……………………….tree in our garden.
(throne/thrown)	An object was ……………………… out of the window.
(leek/leak)	There is a ……………………… in the roof of the shed.
(hymn/him)	The congregation sang a …………………at church today.
(licence/license)	Drivers need to have a ……………… in order to drive.
(here/heir)	The ………………to the British throne is Prince Charles.

VERB FORMATION

Nouns	Verbs
adherence	
accusation	
recovery	
deception	
receipt	
argument	
portrayal	
conversation	
permission	
exemption	

Challenge: *This is one of the most famous Londn landmarks and is associated with an unsuccessful gunpowder plot to kill King James I and destroy the building in 1605?*

Vocabulary Practice Tests (Unit 14)

- **symptoms** (n): clues or signs of illness (e.g. medical)
- **penetrate** (v): to soak through; go through or pierce something
- **invigorate** (v): to liven up or strengthen
- **revoke** (v): to take back something that's been given to someone
- **fatigue** (adj): being tired from physical activities
- **vehement** (adj): being forceful and furious
- **valiant** (adj): brave, courageous
- **associate** (v): to come together as friends
- **outlandish** (adj): strangely peculiar or odd
- **pretentious** (adj): claiming great importance

Vocabulary Practice Test 14

1. After discussing her ……… …………, the doctor gave Rebecca medicine.
2. Some university students have an …………………… style of dressing, with colourful hair and Mohican hairstyles.
3. They ………………….. the club's drinks licence because they broke the law.
4. Dad ……………….. with friends at his golf club during the weekend.
5. A flood in the basement of our house caused water to ……………….the walls.
6. The …………….. Manager was not the owner of the Restaurant; he lied us.
7. Athletes take vitamins and other substances to …………………. their bodies.
8. Diving in the lake to save his friend was a …………………. thing to do.
9. My father complained of feeling …………………. after his day's gardening.
10. Julie was quite ………………about not coming to our fancy dress party.

NOUN FORMATION - More Noun Formation to think about

Verbs	Nouns
invest	
consult	
compel	
penetrate	
revoke	
banish	
embrace	
allocate	
recruit	
depress	

Crossword Puzzle No.3

Across

3. an exact copy of something
4. to have a positive outlook
7. to look like someone
9. booking made in advance of an event
10. based on a limit set by someone

Down

1. to aim for something or have a goal in mind
2. to embarrass or hurt others feelings
5. have the power to lead others
6. relating to society or the general public
8. tease or provoke others

Vocabulary Practice Exercises (Unit 15)

- **condemn** (v): to reject someone; abandon; get rid of someone
- **banish** (v): to send someone away from a place
- **inherit** (v): to get something when someone dies
- **diagnose** (v): when a doctor tells a person what's wrong with them
- **consult** (v): to seek advice from an expert
- **ferocious** (adj): being fierce, savage
- **assault** (v): to threaten or physically harm someone
- **ample** (adj): sufficient, enough
- **convenient** (adj): handy, suitable with little or no trouble
- **apathy** (n): lack of feelings, showing little concern, indifferent

Vocabulary Practice Test 15

1. In history, many witches were ……………………… to die by drowning.
2. We need to …………… a skin specialist about the painful rash on my body.
3. My neighbour's big dog looks quite………………………so I'm scared of it.
4. "You'll have ……………………… time to watch TV, after you've done your homework," said mum.
5. Prince Charles will ……………………… the throne when the Queen dies.
6. The doctor ……………………… …………the patient as having the flu.
7. The police will arrest the man who ……………………… my brother.
8. The wicked fairy ………………………………Snow White into the forest.
9. Despite telling Jane about my loss, there was ……………………… in her behaviour towards me.
10. Living near to my school is quite ………………………, as it only takes me five minutes to get there!

ADJECTIVES FORMATION

Nouns	Adjectives
ignorance	
wonder	
length	
patience	
comfort	
fame	
beauty	

Vocabulary Practice Exercise (Unit 16)

- **attire** (n): the clothes you are wearing
- **dubious** (adj): being unsure, doubtful
- **disperse** (v): to scatter something or a group
- **robust** (adj): strongly built, sturdy
- **calamity** (n): a disaster (e.g. private and public)
- **foresight** (n): the ability or the power to see or make provision for the future
- **concede** (v): to accept or admit something as truth
- **depleted** (adj): used up, reduced or running low
- **comply** (v): to obey or follow
- **invalid** (adj): currently not acceptable

Vocabulary Practice Test 16

1. The Egyptians built many................................ statues and monuments.
2. My library card is now... so I need to renew it.
3. My teacher made the crowd ....from the scene of the fight.
4. Victorian ....was quite different from today's fashion.
5. I am a bit ....about giving money to an unregistered charity.
6. A leader needs to have......................... in order to lead his people well.
7. The champion ....defeat when he was beaten by his opponent.
8. The hurricane caused a .... throughout the country.
9. "You must .... with the school rules," the boy's dad told him.
10. Our food stock is ...., we need to buy some more.

NOUN FORMATION

Verbs	Nouns
expel	
contravene	
accumulate	
antagonise	
detain	
intrude	
intimidate	
compel	
approve	
resemble	

Vocabulary Practice Exercises (Unit 17)

- **manuscript** (n): an unpublished book, written as a draft
- **fellowship** (n): togetherness, showing unity
- **velocity** (n): speed
- **omen** (n): a bid sign
- **disdain** (n): glare at someone with a scornful and hateful look
- **rural** (adj): relating to the countryside
- **tangible** (adj): capable of being felt, solid
- **hindsight** (n): having an understanding of what should have been done after it's happened
- **impose** (v): to force oneself on others
- **animosity** (n): strong dislike or hostility towards others

Vocabulary Practice Test 17

1. The incredible ………………….. of the speedboat caused it to crash.
2. Last week she took her …………………….. to the publishers.
3. There is great ………………. among the team, that's why they always win.
4. "We knew it was a bad …………… when the mirror broke by itself," she said.
5. My uncle and aunt live in a ………………………. area but I live in the city.
6. "With ………………, we could have prepared better for the storm," he said.
7. I have no ………………. towards Jane, although she criticized me.
8. He looked at his boxing opponent with …………………… before striking him down.
9. Peter likes to …………. on others; he invited himself to our house for a week!
10. "We need …………………….. evidence of a crime before we can accuse someone," said the policeman.

SYNONYMS AND OPPOSITES

Words	Synonyms	Antonyms
hypocrite		
inclement		
initial		
peruse		
utilize		
rectify		
excavate		
reprimand		
concession		
symptoms		

Crossword Puzzle No.4

Across
1. to move away from a subject when speaking
3. a strange coincidence
6. a blame or accusation
7. well-known for something bad
8. to offer something in order to please
9. fall heavily to the ground

Down
2. a creation or invention
4. not cared for
5. to hire someone or give them a job
8. to go through a document carefully

Vocabulary Practice Exercises (Unit 18)

- **violate** (v): to break e.g. disobey laws
- **prohibit** (v): to forbid, not allow
- **resuscitate** (v): to revive when apparently dead or unconscious
- **scrutinize** (v): to examine in detail; to look carefully
- **accommodation** (n): the space you occupy to live or work in
- **evade** (v): to manage to avoid someone with slyness
- **insight** (n): having the ability to understand the deeper nature of things
- **incognito** (adj): being undercover, in disguise or assume a false identity
- **outskirts** (n): areas that are away from the centre of a city
- **controversy** (n): a dispute, discussion with conflicting arguments

Vocabulary Practice Test 18

1. The driver was fined for .... road traffic laws.
2. We are .... from walking on rail lines because it's quite dangerous.
3. The ambulance men took 15 minutes to .... the unconscious accident victim.
4. Mum .... the goods carefully before she bought them.
5. This leader has great .... to lead his troops into battle.
6. We live on the .... of London, but go to the city often.
7. The Police are operating .... in the supermarket to catch thieves.
8. There are all kinds of .... surrounding the death of the pop star.
9. He is trying to .... me, because he refuses to answer my calls.
10. Our .... consists of three bedrooms, a living room, bathroom and kitchen.

Add a **Suffix** to the following words:

fashion........ sense........expense...... encourage......... invite....... pain.........

Challenge: *Which famous early 19th century exhibition of revolutionary relics, effigies of public heroes and rogues was brought to Britain and today 200 years later, still brings millions of people into London?*

Vocabulary Practice Exercise (Unit 19)

- **manipulate** (v): to trick some by trying to get your own way
- **recuperate** (v): to recover, get better
- **repercussion** (n): the consequence of an action
- **automation** (n): something that moves by itself
- **adversity** (n): a calamity, disaster, misfortune
- **amiable** (adj: friendly, charming, good-natured,
- **sect** (n): a group or faction
- **unnerve** (v): to lose courage; feel jumpy or nervous
- **mobilize** (v): to gather together for a cause
- **abyss** (n): a pit, gulf, chasm

Vocabulary Practice Test 19

1. Children like to .... their parents especially to get favours.
2. At the stroke of midnight, the noises from the empty house next door........................... me.
3. George ....all his friends to join him in his fight against pollution.
4. It was reported that fighting broke out between two religious ....
5. After the operation, my friend went to .... in her daughter's home.
6. They chased the enemy soldiers into an ...., and claimed the victory.
7. Our world is full of exciting .... due to advance in technology.
8. My neighbours are quite .... people; we get on very well.
9. "Life can be full of ....," my dad's friend said, shaking his head.
10. "He broke the rules, so he must accept the ....," they all said.

Add a Prefix to the following words:
...legal   ...respect   ...annual   ...trust   ...able   ...willing
...captain   ...war   ...cycle   ...mortal   ...known   ...turn

Challenge: *Where will I go? If I want to find inspiration to paint and view Western European traditional paintings from 13th to 20th centuries in London for free!*

Vocabulary Practice Exercise (Unit 20)

- **transition** (n): a move from one stage to the next
- **reimburse** (v): to give back money that has been spent on your behalf
- **fulfill** (v): to do what is promised or expected (task or duty)
- **apprehend** (v): to be caught after a chase or search
- **preside** (v): to lead e.g. a meeting
- **cringe** (v): to shrink in fear or embarrassment
- **formidable** (adj): difficult to defeat or overcome
- **commend** (v): to speak well about someone, recommend or praise them
- **endeavour** (v): to try hard or attempt to do one's best
- **diminutive** (adj): very small size

Vocabulary Practice Test 20

1. They asked me to ………….. over the meeting until the Chairperson arrived.
2. The robber was ……………….. by the police, after a high-speed car chase.
3. The Pygmies are a ………………………. race of people who live in the jungle.
4. I………………….. when the teacher publicly announced my low grades.
5. The boxer's opponent is a ……………………….. challenger.
6. The company will ……………….. our travel costs for attending the meeting.
7. Tom told his mum that he would …………………….. to do his best in the test.
8. Parents have to……………….. their duty by sending their children to school.
9. Secondary schools have……………………….. arrangements to help Year 6 Primary children settle into their new school.
10. "I must …………………….. you on the great efforts you made in your tests, said my teacher.

Challenge: *Where am I?*

In this place you won't bark up the wrong tree!!
You will know your crocodile tooth from the earliest spear in the world, build a volcano and watch it explode? Explore the incredible finds from sites around Britain such as Kent's Cavern in Devon, Pontneywdd in North Wales and Happisburgh in Norfolk.

Vocabulary Practice Exercises (Unit 21)

- **banter** (v): joke around with your friends
- **condone** (v): to encourage or agree to do something bad
- **animated** (adj): done in a lively way, like cartoons
- **vice** (n): a person who is second in command/in charge, like a deputy
- **fractious** (adj): causing a break or detachment
- **stringent** (adj): being strict or severe; harsh
- **transient** (adj): short-lived, temporary
- **oscilate** (v): to swing or sway
- **precarious** (adj): dubious, risky
- **furore** (n): commotion, madness, noisy excitement

Vocabulary Practice Test 21

1. Bullies always ………………………… fights in school.
2. Her strange mood ………………… between happiness and depression!
3. She talked about her holiday experiences in a very………………… way.
4. The boys were ………………… and teasing each other in the playground.
5. Some schools have ……………… rules about uniform and the wearing of hats.
6. There was a ………………… when the champion entered the room; everyone wanted his autograph.
7. The President asked his ………………… to meet with the Prime Minister during his absence.
8. "Our lives on earth are very ………………," said the priest to his congregation.
9. The pop group denied rumours that their band had become ………………
10. It was ……………………for Pete to walk 3 miles to the petrol station so late at night.

NOUN FORMATION

Words	Nouns
retaliate	
apprehend	
precise	
prominent	
contravene	
accumulate	
intrude	
forgive	
affluent	
extravagant	

Crossword Puzzle No.5

Across

5. to dig up, e.g. old ruins
6. not moving or progressing
7. to lie or make up a story
10. extra benefits given to a worker apart from his salary

Down

1. living together
2. to soak through or pierce something
3. to put money into a business or project
4. to punish
8. to take back something that's been given
9. to force something to do something

Vocabulary Practice Exercises (Unit 22)

- **somber** (adj): being sad or sorrowful
- **intoxicated** (adj): being drunk
- **antagonize** (v): to taunt, scare or tease
- **dupe** (v): to trick or fool someone
- **dismal** (adj): unpleasant or bad conditions (weather)
- **insipid** (adj): silly, senseless, uninteresting
- **volatile** (adj): changeable, unsteady, reckless
- **autonomous** (adj): independent, self-determined
- **succinct** (adj): clear and concise
- **docile** (adj): easily led, submissive

Vocabulary Practice Test 22

1. The police stopped a driver because he was driving while ....
2. He said it was .... logic to have his desert before eating his dinner!
3. "Your expressions are quite .... in your story," he said.
4. Having lost his money, the boy was in a .... mood all afternoon.
5. The weather has been quite ....lately; too much wind and rain.
6. The kidnapping of the girls created a very .... situation for rescuers.
7. Shoppers sometimes get .... when buying from dishonest traders.
8. The new-comers to the boarding school quickly learnt how to be .... while competing to achieve the top awards.
9. Bullies like to .... their victims.
10. The .... boy took the cigarettes from his friends and smoked them.

ADJECTIVE FORMATION

Words	Adjectives
distinct	
fury	
precision	
prominence	
jubilee	
accumulation	
intruder	
scorn	
affluence	
extravagance	

Vocabulary Practice Exercises (Unit 23)

- **prominent** (adj): a place that is very noticeable or important
- **intuition** (n): a strong sense of knowing or having an instinct about things
- **contravene** (v): to disobey or break e.g. rules or laws
- **writhe** (v): to twist in pain
- **replenish** (v): to restock or refill
- **swindle** (v): to dupe or trick others and take what is theirs
- **vandalise** (v): to destroy, needlessly
- **penultimate** (adj): the one coming before the last
- **evict** (v): to kick out, to get rid of someone from a building
- **anecdote** (n): a story used to illustrate a point

Vocabulary Practice Test 23

1. The Queen's portrait hangs in a .... place in the Prime Minister's office.
2. Many drivers .... the law by driving through red lights.
3. The old lady was .... out of her pension and savings by a dishonest salesman.
4. "It's a criminal offence to .... other people's property," he said.
5. It is said that women have very strong ....
6. I found the answer to the question in the .... verse of the poem.
7. We have to .... our food-stock as we are running out of food.
8. My neighbour was .... from his home for not paying his rent.
9. Our teacher always gives us an .... when she explains our new vocabulary words.
10. He .... in pain when he was punched in the stomach.

Challenge:
Which famous London visitor attraction can give you a panoramic learning across the curriculum to include; geography, history, architecture, technology, engineering, literacy, Maths, culture and community; while hanging in the air and revolving at 360 degrees

Vocabulary Practice Exercise (Unit 24)

- **abundance** (n): a large amount
- **sever** (v): to cut off from a joint
- **accumulate** (v): to amass or gather over a period of time
- **tedious** (adj): long and boring
- **vociferous** (adj): loud, noisy
- **cajole** (v): to flatter, tempt, coax, encourage
- **frenzied** (adj): happening in a crazy or raging manner
- **dawdle** (v): to loiter, delay, lag behind
- **chaffing** (v): to mock, jeer, ridicule
- **deterrent** (n): something that helps to prevent something from happening

Vocabulary Practice Test 24

1. Our apple tree grew in .... last summer, so we gave some away.

2. We begged and .... Sally to go to the cinema with us but she refused!

3. My brother has .... a lot of foreign stamps.

4. The boys .... on his way home from school, causing his mother to worry.

5. The large dog made a .... attack on another dog as it passed by.

6. We installed an alarm in our house to act as a .... to burglars.

7. Having to copy 10 pages of this story by hand is quite ....

8. The class became .... when the teacher announced that they would go to a theme park for a day's outing.

9. The butcher .... the meat from the joints, then weighed the pieces for his customers.

10. Despite the .... from his friends, Dillon insisted that he would sing and dance on stage to a Michael Jackson song.

Challenge: *Fancy flying?*
Where will you need to go to feel what it's like to fly with the Red Arrows or blast off into space on an Apollo space mission in 3D and 4D simulators. Put 4 London double-decker buses together, that's how tall the screen is where you can interactively experience this.

Crossword Puzzle No.6

Across

3. to seek advice from an expert
4. clothes you are wearing
6. a place of learning for advanced education
8. to hug someone
9. to mend, fix or put something right

Down

1. doubtful, uncertain
2. loneliness
5. the body of a dead person
6. a person pretending to be someone they are not
7. a quiet and peaceful e.g. place

Vocabulary Practice Exercise (Unit 25)

- **vengeance** (n): revenge
- **utilize** (v): to use up e.g. time
- **treacherous** (adj): untrustworthy, disloyal, deceitful
- **ominous** (adj): threatening, a bad sign
- **rudimentary** (adj): elementary, or the beginning stages
- **delve** (v): to act on something straight away
- **inauguration** (n): the beginning ceremony, start; an official opening,
- **plausible** (adj): believable, credible, likely
- **trudge** (v): to walk heavily or wearily
- **nuisance** (n): a bother, bore, annoyance

Vocabulary Practice Test 25

1. "Please ……………………. your time wisely," said the supervisor, "You only have ten minutes left."

2. We …………………………. into our homework straight after school, so we could watch a film later.

3. The rescue team ………………… through heavy snow to help the stranded driver.

4. My neighbours are a ……………………….; they play loud music too late at night.

5. Millions of people around the world watched the ……………………….. of the American President.

6. He swore he would take out ……………………… on his neighbour for deliberately crashing into his car.

7. "Your story is quite …………… I would like to interview you," said the reporter.

8. When the goal-keeper injured his leg, it was an ……………………….. sign that the team probably would not win the match.

9. "These are the……………………….. techniques for story-writing, now you need to learn them for a test next week," the teacher announced.

10. They searched for the missing plane in …………………………… seas to locate the black box.

Challenge:
What is the name of the largest and most stunning Gothic cathedral in Northern England, which began construction around 1230 and finished in 1472?

Vocabulary Practice Exercises (Unit 26)

- **fragment** (n): broken pieces
- **summit** (n): at the very top (e.g. mountain)
- **annual** (adj): happening every year
- **peril** (n): danger
- **affluent** (adj): very rich, wealthy
- **breach** (n): a break in a law or promise
- **morality** (n): a standard that is good and accepted in life by society
- **hygienic** (adj): the practice of cleanliness and good health
- **distended** (adj): greatly stretched or to swell from the inside e.g. belly
- **anxiety** (n): worry and uneasiness

Vocabulary Practice Test 26

1. The glass fell and broke into ....
2. The Queen is ...., so she can buy anything she wants!
3. Your life will be in .... if you walk on the train track.
4. The drunk driver is in .... of road traffic laws.
5. The poor starving children had .... stomachs.
6. Our school has an .... sports day.
7. "The state of ....among young people in the country is questionable," said the speaker to the Members of Parliament.
8. Washing your hands after toilet use is a good .... practice.
9. His face was full of .... as they came to end of the tennis match.
10. Climbers tried to each the .... of the mountain before dark.

MORE PREFIXES TO LEARN

Prefixes	Meaning	Examples
ante	before	antecedent
contra	against	contrary, contradict
inter	between	international, interval
trans	across	transport, transfer
circum	round	circumference
fore	before	forecast, foretell
vice	instead	Vice-President, Vice-captain

Vocabulary Practice Exercises (Unit 27)

- **rapid** (adj): happing very quickly
- **sorrow** (n): feeling of sadness
- **opportunity** (n): a chance given to someone
- **compel** (v): to force someone to do something
- **massive** (adj): a huge size
- **scared** (adj): feeling afraid
- **abundant** (adj): lots, a huge amount
- **extravagant** (adj): spend a lot of money easily
- **saunter** (v): to walk in a leisurely or idle way
- **engulf** (v): to overwhelm, to move rapidly e.g. fire, water

Vocabulary Practice Test 27

1. The little boy was ………………… to go near the big dog.
2. We built a …………………… sandcastle on the beach in Spain.
3. "I am giving you an ………………. to tell me what happened," said mum.
4. That big boy …………………. me to give him my lunch money.
5. The man who won the lottery was very ……………………… with his money; he bought a boat, a motorbike and three fast cars.
6. Our plum tree grew an…………………….. amount of plums last year.
7. A fire started in the basement, then ……………………. the entire building.
8. The cold water runs ………………… from the tap into the bathtub.
9. Sally was full of …………………….. after her pet rabbit died.
10. The young couple laughed and talked as they …………………… hand-in-hand around the park.

Challenge: *Where am I?*
This is one of the world's most famous buildings, with 900 years of history, having been home to prisoners, palace for royalty, and those without heads! There are jewels here which are described as having a relationship with the "Crown."

Vocabulary Practice Exercise (Unit 28)

- **console** (v): to comfort someone in a time of suffering
- **errand** (n): a little job that you go and do for someone
- **domesticated** (adj): trained for life in the home e.g. animals
- **merchandise** (n): goods for sale
- **extrovert** (adj): a bold and audacious personality
- **culminate** (v): to reach the highest point, to bring to a head
- **phony** (adj): something that is fake, not genuine
- **testimony** (n): a declaration of truth or fact
- **undisputed** (adj): uncontested, unbeatable
- **customary** (n): a common habit

Vocabulary Practice Test 28

1. Mum sent me on an .... to the corner shop, to buy bread.
2. Muhammad Ali is the ....boxing champion of the world.
3. We had to .... Andrew because he lost his pet hamster.
4. After their ordeal, each kidnapped victim gave a .... of what happened.
5. Some young people display signs of .... behaviour to cover up for some of their fears.
6. Dogs and cats are .... animals.
7. Some market have .... traders selling replica goods.
8. Our practice matches .... in a contest between the two best players.
9. All the .... in the warehouse was damaged by a flood.
10. It is .... to give a toast to the Queen at very official functions.

NOUN FORMATION

Words	Nouns
expert	
repatriate	
presume	
intimidate	
censor	
dejected	
acquire	
empower	
proceed	
intend	

Crossword Puzzle No.7

Across

5. speed

6. to collect and keep or store things

7. to glare at someone with a scorn

8. to examine something carefully

9. neat and tidy, paying attention to details

10. to tell a person what is medically wrong with them

Down

1. to break or disobey the law

2. to take revenge

3. to forbid or not allow

4. the consequence of an action

Vocabulary Practice Exercise (Unit 29)

- **introvert** (n): a person who is shy and quiet
- **aroma** (n): the smell of food or drink
- **odour** (n): an unpleasant smell
- **scent** (n): a very pleasant smell e.g. perfume
- **solidarity** (n); togetherness, a united group of people with similar interests
- **novice** (n): a beginner, or new to something
- **appropriate** (adj): suitable, correctly suited
- **indecision** (n): hesitation, doubts, unable to make up your mind
- **emancipate** (v): to liberate or free someone or something
- **incision** (n): a cut or an opening (e.g. done by a doctor in surgery)

Vocabulary Practice Test 29

1. The staff at our school showed ……………………………by joining the strike.
2. "I like the ………………………………. of your new perfume," said Amy.
3. "As a ……………… ……….of this game, I don't expect to win," she warned.
4. It is not ……………………… for adults to use bad language in front of children.
5. The doctor made an ……………… below her left rib, then operated on the child.
6. The new girl seems to be an ……………………… as she doesn't want to be part of any group.
7. As I entered our house, the ……………………… of mum's cooking filled the air.
8. "Put your trainers outside to get rid of the ………………………," said dad.
9. The plantation owners had to ……………………………. the slaves in 1836.
10. "I am plagued by ……………………… as to whether to travel by sea or air," she moaned.

SYNONYMS AND OPPOSITES

Words	Synonyms	Antonyms
permanent		
timid		
concise		
contest		
forbid		
solemn		
immense		
indolent		
authorize		

Vocabulary Practice Exercise (Unit 30)

- **arrogant** (adj): to think you are better than others
- **notify** (v): to inform or tell about something
- **obstruct** (v): to block someone or to be in their way
- **stranded** (adj): being stuck and left without support or help
- **wound** (v): to hurt or injure yourself
- **stray** (adj): abandon, deserted, left without help
- **regiment** (n): a group of people (as in the army, police)
- **prior** (adj): happening before an event
- **audible** (adj): can be heard clearly, a distinct sound
- **imperfections** (n): not perfect having faults or weaknesses,

Vocabulary Practice Test 30

1. She fell off the swing and ……………………… herself.
2. It is …………… to believe you are better than absolutely everyone.
3. If you stand in the train doorway you will ………………… the doors from closing.
4. We always feed a ………………… cat when it comes into our garden.
5. He apologized for his poor attitude and the ………………… of his behaviour.
6. The children washed their hands………………… to having their lunch.
7. The Scottish …………………… fought bravely against the foreign army.
8. The noise from an argument in the street was ………… ………… in my room.
9. Mum has to ………………… my teacher that I would be absent from school.
10 We were ……………………… in Central London with no money when we missed the last train home.

Challenge: *Want to touch a 4.5 billion-year old meteorite?*
You will need to go to this place of four, whose names associated with "royalty" and "time". You can also shoot down a dastardly pirate ship and discover stories about Britain's encounter with the world at sea.

Vocabulary Practice Exercise (Unit 31)

- **modern** (adj): not old
- **depart** (v): to leave a place
- **broad** (adj): wide
- **hind** (adj): at the back or the rear e.g. legs
- **exemplary** (adj): a perfect example
- **steadfast** (adj): being firm, fixed, resolute, unchanging
- **blemish** (n): a defect, flaw or spot
- **efficacious** (adj): very effective
- **impeccable** (adj): of high standard or quality
- **indelible** (adj): can't be erased or removed

Vocabulary Practice Test 31

1. The pilot said that the plane will now .... from Heathrow Airport for New York.
2. There are .... fashion stores throughout London.
3. His service is ...., so we recommended him to a friend.
4. "That medicine is quite ...., I feel much better," said the patient.
5. "Our holiday experience has left an ....mark on my mind," said the man to his wife.
6. His written speech has no ...., I'm sure it will make a great impact on his audience.
7. "Your behaviour has been .... this term," my teacher told me.
8. I saw one ....table among two rectangular ones in the dining room.
9. The dog was limping because it had a thorn in its .... leg.
10. "Whatever happens during this battle, you must be ....," said the Army General advisedly to his men.

SYNONYMS

Words	Synonym
insolent	
magnanimous	
hoax	
bereavement	
allegation	

Challenge: *Can you guess whose famous home in London has 775 rooms? And you're invited to a famous event there all year round!*

Crossword Puzzle No.8

Across

4. lively and exciting

5. unpleasant conditions e.g. weather

6. someone who is learning a job from an experience person

10. planned in advance

Down

1. being drunk from alcohol

2. to encourage someone to do something bad

3. suitable or helps a situation e.g. atmosphere

7. like a king or queen

8. to trick or fool someone

9. gather or collect or accumulate

Vocabulary Practice Exercise (Unit 32)

- **infamous** (adj): well-known for something bad, notorious
- **recluse** – an isolated person shut off from the world (sometimes for religious reasons)
- **compensate** (v): to pay for a loss or damage done
- **garrulous** (adj): very talkative, chatty
- **desist** (v): to stop an action that you are doing
- **alleviate** (v): to relieve or get rid of e.g. an emotion – pain, stress
- **empower** (v): to influence, motivate or give power to someone
- **amplify** (v): to make sound louder
- **serene** (adj): very quiet and calm, tranquil
- **composure** (n): confidence and calm attitude

Vocabulary Practice Test 32

1. The old lady had become a ....; she had no friends or family.
2. "I need to .... you for the damage I did to your garden fence," his neighbour told him.
3. Children are naturally... .... but are usually told to be quiet.
4. "You must ....from shouting," said the teacher.
5. She sat in the empty church feeling .... and confident.
6. The Conference speaker has......................... me to write an action plan.
7. "I admire your.................... in the midst of your awful situation," said Tom.
8. We needed something to .... the sound in the hall so that everyone can hear the performers on stage.
9. She took a pain-killer to .... her headache.
10. Historically, Jack-the-Ripper is an .... character.

VERB FORMATION

Nouns	Verbs
instigation	
consumption	
receipt	
aspiration	
presumption	
preoccupation	
perseverance	
deflation	
recollection	
permission	

Vocabulary Practice Exercise (Unit 33)

- **ascent** (n): a climb upwards
- **obtain** (v): to go and get
- **vendor** (n): a person who sells on the street or in a market
- **extinguish** (v):– to put out (e.g. pour water on fire)
- **seize** (v): to take something by force
- **altitude** (n): the height especially above sea level
- **reluctant** (adj): being hesitant or unsure
- **reprimand** (v): to punish someone
- **endangered** (adj): at risk or in danger
- **sullen** (adj): moody, silent, gloomy, dull

Vocabulary Practice Test 33

1. The fire men struggled to ……………………….. the fire.
2. His goods were ……………………. because he had not paid his bill.
3. I am …………………..to drive into central London, so I'll take the train.
4. After taking off, the plane made a steady ………………..to 10,000 feet high.
5. "You will be ……………………. for fighting in school," said the boy's dad.
6. The panda bear is an ……………………………………….. specie.
7. She looked …………………….. after she broke up with her best friend.
8. I need to ……………………. a travel ticket before I leave for my journey.
9. The ……………………….. has decided not to sell his house.
10. Planes fly at ………………..of over 20,000 feet over the Atlantic Ocean.

NOUN FORMATION

Words	Nouns
amend	
distract	
dedicate	
delegate	
generous	
seize	
ascend	

Challenge: *Where can you do this?*
Experience life as a 17th and 18th century royal courtier, whilst exploring the magnificent King's and Queen's State Apartments adorned with remarkable paintings from the Royal Collection. You can also see where Queen Victoria lived as a child, and where the spotlight on 20th century young royals remain today.

Vocabulary Practice Exercise (Unit 34)

- **longevity** (n): having long life
- **cosmopolitan** (adj): having an interest in all parts of the world, not limited to one nationality
- **flotsam & jetsam** (n): bits of objects floating in the sea after a wreckage
- **contract** (v): to make smaller in size
- **neglect** (v): to not care or look after something or someone
- **extol** (v): to praise, celebrate or applaud someone
- **orthodox** (adj): following established behaviour, opinions or practices
- **substantial** (adj): considerable size, amount or value
- **lavish** (adj): to give or spend a generous amount, freely on someone
- **vibrant** (adj): very energetic, lively or bright

Vocabulary Practice Test 34

1. Nelson Mandela had ....; he was more than 95 years when he died.
2. This rubber band can expand to twice its length, then ....
3. After wining the lottery, my neighbours .... a huge sum of money on their children by buying them numerous toys and games.
4. The colours of school uniforms in Britain are definitely not ....
5. The City of London is very .... but expensive to live in.
6. At the deceased Mayor funeral, the speaker.......................... the Mayor's past generosity and charitable works.
7. My neighbour has ....his garden, due to his painful legs.
8. The student borrowed a .... amount of money to last him for three years at university.
9. ....and .... were found floating in the sea after two ships collided.
10. Many religions do not follow British .... forms of worship.

Challenge:
Do you know where to find the residence of George II daughters and also family home of George III, where everything is still just as it was during King George's reign?

Vocabulary Practice Exercise (Unit 35)

- **insolent** (adj); very rude
- **bi-annual** (adj): taking place twice a year
- **frock** (n): a dress
- **eminent** (adj): a very important or distinguished person
- **nauseous** (adj): to feel like vomiting
- **clemency** (n): a pardon, forgiveness given to someone
- **stingy** (adj): being very mean, not generous
- **sabotage** (v): to deliberately damage or cause disruption by enemies
- **tempestuous** (adj): stormy, like a hurricane
- **suburbs** (n): a residential district away from a town or city; the outskirts,

Vocabulary Practice Test 35

1. Ladies wore very long .... in Victorian times.
2. "We have an .... visitor in our school," said the Head teacher.
3. The President offered the criminal ...., just as he was about to be hung; due to new evidence that proves his innocence.
4. The .... boy got detention during break time.
5. Susan and George have a very .... relationship, so they have finally decided to split up.
6. The children live in the .... of London, so they travel to school by train.
7. Max is quite a .... man who hoards his money and pretends to be poor.
8. We have a special .... edition of the school magazine in our library.
9. Workers planned to .... their company but were caught by their boss who called the police.
10. "Travelling on boats and ships make me feel ....," said Sue.

NOUN FORMATION

Words	Nouns
impudent	
enrich	
diagnose	
disfigure	
adhere	
compensate	
interact	

Crossword Puzzle No.9

Across
4. the smell of food cooking
6. a beginner/new to something
7. spend a lot of money easily
8. rich or wealthy
10. very lazy

Down
1. happening soon
2. bad weather conditions
3. in a noticeable place
5. goods for sale
9. very tiny

Vocabulary Practice Exercise (Unit 36)

- **cravat** (n): a tie
- **locate** (v): to find the position of something
- **detain** (v): to be kept back for a reason, held by someone in authority
- **retire** (v): to leave a job after being in it for a very long time
- **elect** (v): to choose
- **resign** (v): to write a letter stating that you are leaving a job
- **expedite** (v): to speed up the process of doing something
- **quaint** (adj): being attractive in an old-fashioned style
- **delegate** (v): to give power to someone or share responsibility
- **academic** (adj): scholarly, relating to school, college or university

Vocabulary Practice Test 36

1. Our Head teacher, who has been at our school for 40 years, is going to ………………………….. at the end of the school year.
2. The police will …………………..you if they have lots of questions to ask you.
3. The Director has both………………………. qualifications and life skills.
4. In Victorian times men wore ……………………., but today we call them ties.
5. This 35 year old, decorative, jewelry box is quite …………………………
6. They are going to ………………… the place where the helicopter crashed.
7. I will need to ……………… various responsibilities to my staff in my absence.
8. They are going to ……………………… Pradeep as the new football captain.
9. Mr. Jones does not like his job so he is going to ……………………….
10. The Passport Office will need to ………………………… my passport application; I need to travel urgently.

SYNONYMS AND OPPOSITES

Words	Synonyms	Opposites
despise		
imminent		
obsolete		
squander		
concise		
outskirts		
diligent		
publicise		
stubborn		
gloat		

Vocabulary Practice Exercise (Unit 37)

- **adhere** (v): to stick to or obey e.g. rules
- **embezzle** (v): when an employee steals money from his/her company
- **trickster** (n): a person who deceives or tricks others
- **prolific** (adj): producing an abundant amount
- **prosecute** (v): to bring legal action against someone e.g. in a court of law
- **denomination** (n): a type of religious group
- **furtive** (adj): being sly, stealthy, secretive
- **radiant** (adj): brilliant, dazzling, shining
- **inflict** (v): to impose pain or suffering on someone
- **accessible** (adj): easy to reach or get to something

Vocabulary Practice Test 37

1. When you travel you must ……………….to the rules of the country you are in.
2. Buckingham Palace is quite ……………………….. to the general public.
3. Many people belong to the Church of England …………………….
4. The Accountant was sent to jail because he …………………….. the company's money.
5. I am going to ……………………….. my neighbour for breaking into my home.
6. People described him as a confidence ………………..; he also robbed houses.
7. That bully ………………….. pain on others by tormenting and fighting them.
8. My father is a ……………………. writer, who has written several books.
9. The men saw a …………………………. light in the sky and thought it might be a spaceship.
10. The girl's admirer took ……………………. glances at her when she was not looking.

NOUN FORMATION

Words	Nouns
animated	
locate	
retire	
elect	
resign	
deviate	
betray	
hazard	

Challenge: *Where in England would you find the Cerne Abbas Giant?*

Vocabulary Practice Exercises (Unit 38)

- **generosity** (n): unselfishness, not mean
- **majority** (n): the most in a group
- **hazardous** (adj): dangerous or risky
- **exodus** (n): the departure or exit of a lot of people at once
- **betrayal** (n): to let someone down badly
- **influence** (v): to have the power to affect others
- **sacrifice** (v): to offer something valuable for something more important
- **prophesy** (v): to predict the future
- **inevitable** (adj): sure to happen
- **garner** (v): to gather, collect, reserve or hoard

Vocabulary Practice Test 38

1. Marjorie's ....was well-known among the poor people of her neighbourhood.
2. The tennis player plans to .... his strength in order to win the next match.
3. The sailors ....their belongings in order to keep their boat afloat.
4. The civil war caused an .... of people to leave the city and go into the countryside.
5. The class monitor, has a great .... on the rest of the class.
6. It is .... that all humans will die at some point.
7. My friend talks about the .... that her brother suffered by an older boy in school.
8. A man is going to .... about the country's future on live television tonight.
9. Wet floors can sometimes be ...., so you must take care.
10. The .... of children in our class can speak two languages.

Challenge:
Which bridge, built in 1894, is one of London's most recognizable landmarks and also one of the most famous bridges in the world? It spans the River Thames and is next to the Tower of London.

Crossword Puzzle No.10

Across
3. very talkative
5. an escaped prisoner
7. long life
9. to relieve
10. trick or fool someone

Down
1. an unpleasant smell
2. to give a reason for something
4. to get better or recover
6. to plan in secret
8. to inform or let someone know something

Vocabulary Practice Exercises (Unit 39)

- **feasible** (adj); workable, likely to succeed
- **conducive** (adj): suitable an environment that helps or supports something
- **irrational** (adj): acting without reason or logic; absurd
- **regress** (v): to become worse, after a period of progress
- **incongruous** (adj): lacking harmony, parts don't agree
- **frailty** (n): being physically weak as in old age
- **incisive** (adj): a personality that is sharp and to the point; very decisive
- **sober** (adj): not drunk, free of alcohol intake
- **monumental** (adj): huge and challenging
- **cyclical** (adj): happening in cycles

Vocabulary Practice Test 39

1. The mountain climbers had a ………………………… task ahead of them, aiming for their 2,500ft victory.
2. After some threats by gang members, the boy's behaviour became quiet and ………………………… .
3. Studying in the library is ………………………… to learning.
4. Our four seasons are …………………; so are the changes from birth to death.
5. The patient got better after his operation; luckily he did not ………………………
6. Darren, the group's driver, was the only one who was ……………………… after the party.
7. The plan to build a new supermarket is ………………………; we must start soon.
8. Our camp leader was quite …………………, when he changed our travel plans.
9. The two choirs' chaotic attempts to rehearse for the show were quite …………………………
10. Due to his …………………, Mr. Brown gave up his flat to live with his son.

Form **Adverbs** from the following words

1. obey	…………………………	7. abundant	…………………………
2. impudent	…………………………	8. incredible	…………………………
3. immediate	…………………………	9. painful	…………………………
4. vigorous	…………………………	10. incessant	…………………………
5. clumsy	…………………………	11. potential	…………………………
6. serious	…………………………	12. justifiable	…………………………

Challenge: *What and where is The Royal Mews?*

Vocabulary Practice Exercise (Unit 40)

- **despicable** (adj): horrible, disgusting
- **acquaintance** (n): a friend, someone you know
- **potential** (n): the talent or ability to do well
- **campaign** (n): a group of people who agree to fight for a cause
- **commitment** (n): something that you make a great effort to do
- **vacancy** (n): an empty space or opportunity available for a job
- **obsolete** (adj): old and out of date, no longer in use
- **demolish** (v): to destroy or break down
- **conspire** (v): to plan something in secret
- **stereotype** (v): to categorise a person in a negative way

Vocabulary Practice Test 40

1. They joined the .... against delinquents who vandalise our streets.
2. My teacher says that I have the .... to do well in my exam.
3. She made a .... to help me with my work during the summer holidays.
4. "Excuse me, I am here to find out about the .... you have for a Shop Assistant," the man said.
5. Our school computers are now ...., so we need new ones.
6. Some Serial killers commit .... crimes.
7. I have many .... but a few really close friends.
8. The Council has decided to .... a number of old buildings.
9. It is claimed that some people .... to kill the Leader.
10. It is quite unfair to .... all young people as delinquents.

FORM VERB FROM THESE WORDS

Words	Verbs
recurrence	
suspension	
enchantment	
preoccupation	
abstention	
economy	
improvisation	
perseverance	
authorization	
nomination	

Vocabulary Practice Exercise (Unit 41)

- **industrious** (adj): very hard-working, diligent
- **provoke** (v): to tease or taunt someone
- **collision** (n): a head-on crash involving vehicles
- **pioneer** (n): the first person to invent or create something
- **accomplish** (v): to achieve or complete something
- **contemplate** (v): to decide or consider doing something
- **recruit** (v): to give someone a job
- **solemn** (n): serious, somber or gloomy
- **formalize** (v): to put in writing, to make official or legal
- **premeditated** (adj): not an accident; an action that is planned in advance

Vocabulary Practice Test 41

1. The new boy was ……………………..by the school bully so he fought back.
2. James is an …………………………. student who always does his work.
3. Luckily, the ……………………. was not fatal; both drivers survived the crash.
4. You will need to ……………………. the offer you made to me on the telephone.
5. The Wright Brothers were ……………………… of the airplane.
6. McDonald Restaurants plan to ……………………. 50 students this summer.
7. The Royal Wedding last April, was a ……………………………. occasion.
8. "I will relax only when I have ……………………. all my tasks for today," he said.
9. Tom is ………………. ……….whether to go to Central London by bus or train.
10. In the TV crime drama, a man was jailed for the ………………………. murder of his friend.

SYNONYMS AND OPPOSITES

Words	Synonyms	Opposites
replenish		
condense		
motivate		
notify		
obstruct		
depart		
deceive		
retain		
conspire		

Vocabulary Practice Exercise (Unit 42)

- **frank** (adj): free and direct in expressing yourself
- **commute** (v): to travel by train daily from a suburban home to a city office
- **fortitude** (n): showing great courage in adversity
- **concise** (adj): being clear, accurate and to the point
- **spruce** (v): to smarten up, looking clean and tidy
- **meager** (adj): very thin, looking emaciated
- **stale** (adj): no longer fresh (e.g. food)
- **eavesdrop** (v): to listen secretly to a private conversation
- **inferno** (n): a devastating fire
- **humdrum** (adj): dull, ordinary, boring

Vocabulary Practice Test 42

1. The block of flats which were on fire, looked like a towering ....
2. Michael showed great ....; having survived a severe blizzard on a mountain for 5 days.
3. We are .... up our flat because we are expecting visitors!
4. They cooked this food two days ago, so it is now ....
5. My friend's dog looks quite ...., it seems unwell.
6. Mum .... to work on the over-ground train to London every day.
7. "I'm being .... with you," said Andrew, "You seem unhappy about something!"
8. "Do not .... on my conversation," the girl warned her little sister.
9. The retired sailor now leads a very .... life.
10. Her answers to the exams questions were very ....

Give another word for the following

1. fatigue	....	7. remedy	....
2. obstinate	....	8. sever	....
3. wretched	....	9. consume	....
4. residence	....	10. statutory	....
5. affectionate	....	11. concise	....
6. garrulous	....	12. solitude	....

Do you know? *Which famous construction of stone (built around 3100BC), took more than thirty million hours of labour. Speculation – some say it was built for human sacrifice, others say for astronomy and worship of the moon and sun.*

Crossword Puzzle No.11

Across

3. stick to something or obey e.g. rules
5. destroy or breakdown
6. dangerous or risky
7. having a negative outlook on life
9. old and out of date, no longer in use

Down

1. when an employee steals money from his company
2. tease or make someone angry
3. a friend, someone you know
4. very hardworking
8. very rude

© 2018 Roselle Thompson   Vocabulary Skills for Practical Learning – Volume 1

Vocabulary Practice Exercise (Unit 43)

- **immobilize** (v) – to prevent something from moving
- **injustice** (n): the practice of being unfair or producing an unjust act
- **hearty** (adj): warm and friendly
- **temerity** (n): a state of being rash, showing boldness
- **predecessor** (n): the former holder of a position or office
- **tattle** (n): gossip, idle chatter
- **heckle** (v): to harass a speaker with questions or taunts
- **statistics** (n): information which is analysed and expressed in numbers
- **inventory** (n): an itemized list of goods or property
- **inundated** (v): to be flooded with something; overwhelmed e.g. fan letters or phone calls

Vocabulary Practice Test 43

1. Many people like to .... about others, especially when they are idle.
2. We gave our guests a .... welcome to our meeting.
3. Mandy cheated but had the ....to complain of her low test marks.
4. Our car was ....when they clamped it.
5. According to ...., more students pass GCSE exams than fail them.
6. Members of the audience .... the speaker as he walked off the stage.
7. The Landlord took an ....of the flat's contents before he rented it.
8. The winner of the talent show was .... with calls and letters.
9. Our new chairman's .... was a part-owner in the company.
10. She talked of the .... she suffered from the court.

SYNONYMS AND OPPOSITES

Words	Synonyms	Antonyms
contemplate		
fabricate		
accept		
abstain		
deliberate		
occupation		
speculate		
restrict		
animated		
presume		

Vocabulary Practice Exercise (Unit 44)

- **instigate** (v): to stir up something; to start trouble
- **foe** (n): an enemy
- **agenda** (n): a list of things to be discussed at a meeting
- **authentic** (adj): genuine, not false or copied
- **committee** (n): a group of people in a meeting, (selected to do something)
- **territory** (n): a marked-off area
- **pamper** (v): to spoil someone or give too much attention
- **emulate** (v): to imitate, or compete by trying to do better than someone
- **nee** (n): a woman's surname before she gets married
- **intersperse** (v): to scatter or insert among other things

Vocabulary Practice Test 44

1. Naughty children ………………………… fights in the playground.
2. The meeting was a disaster because there was no …………………… to guide us.
3. The young trainee tries to ………………… the actions of his boss in his absence.
4. Travelling to different countries is a wonderful way to sample many types of ……………………… cuisines.
5. Her yellow floral arrangement was …………………… with red and white roses.
6. Sarah's mum ………………… her at home, now she refuses to get her own book.
7. They shot the animal, believing it to be a ……………………but it was friendly.
8. Some professional women still use their ………………………, despite being married.
9. Many animals protect their ………………… by fighting off others that came near.
10. The company's finance ……………………… has agreed that each worker will get a £50 bonus next Christmas.

VERB FORMATION

Words	Verbs
pretext	
innovation	
instigation	
ignition	
conspiracy	
demolition	
provocation	
intervention	
recruitment	
resignation	

Vocabulary Practice Exercise (Unit 45)

- **democracy** (n): a government that is selected or chosen by its people
- **consume** (v): to take in as food, to eat/drink up
- **economy** (n): the system of managing a country
- **monarch** (n): a queen or king
- **immense** (adj): unusually large, huge
- **candidate** (n): someone taking an exam, or attending a conference
- **ramification** (n): the consequence or result of an action
- **eccentric** (adj): odd, unconventional in manner and dress
- **communal** (adj): shared by everyone; belonging to the community
- **prodigy** (n): someone or something you marvel at, that's extraordinary

Vocabulary Practice Test 45

1. I am a .... for the 11+ English exams which is being held tomorrow.
2. The Prime Minister spoke about the country's .... to the House of Commons.
3. My neighbour and I share a .... driveway to park our cars.
4. "This government is a ....," the Minister stressed, "So we would like your views."
5. Britain's .... recently celebrated her Diamond Jubilee.
6. The priest told the drunk man that he should not .... any more alcohol.
7. The annual festival brought .... crowds to the local town.
8. The musical genius is incessantly training his .... to become the world's best musician.
9. The doctor told his patient to consider the .... of his coming heart surgery.
10. We photographed an .... man dressed in his 60 year soldier's uniform wandering aimlessly on the High Street.

Challenge:
Where is thought to be the most eccentric village in the UK? It was constructed by Sir Clough Williams-Ellis between 1925 and 1975, with a hotel, holiday cottages, a teashop and a restaurant!!

Crossword Puzzle No.12

Across

1. a king or queen
4. a list of things to be discussed at a meeting
7. to prevent something from moving
8. to consider or decide
9. to stir up trouble

Down

2. to take in as food, eat/drink
3. to put in writing, make official or legal
5. achieve or complete something
6. to get involved in something that's happening
8. brief and to the point

Vocabulary Practice Exercise (Unit 46)

- **congestion** (n): traffic jam, overcrowded roads with lots of vehicles
- **feat** (n): an incredible performance
- **retain** (v): to keep something safely
- **tepid** (adj): slightly warm
- **oust** (v): to force someone out of their position e.g. job
- **gratitude** (n): being thankful for favours received
- **embark** (v): to go on board a ship, train, bus or plane
- **eliminate** (v): to get rid of completely e.g. a competition
- **mammoth** (adj): huge or enormous
- **alight** (v): to get off from a bus, train, plan, ship

Vocabulary Practice Test 46

1. I wash my face in .... water each day.

2. The team faced a .... task, running a mile in the obstacle race.

3. "Please .... your receipt," said the Cashier, "In case you want to bring this toy back."

4. Many incredible .... were performed on a high rope at the circus last night.

5. Mum expressed her ....to my teachers for helping me with my work.

6. The bus conductor told the passengers to ...., as the bus had broken down.

7. All passengers to New York were told to .... on their plane.

8. There was an accident on the High Street, and this caused .... for many hours.

9. The champion tennis player was .... by his opponent in the second match.

10. The army had planned to .... their country's leader, but their plans were unsuccessful.

Challenge: *Do you know the name of this place?*
It is popularly called "Britain's Magical Waterland". They are a series of rivers and lakes which are navigable; less than 4 metres deep and totaling 303 kilometres. What is it called?

Vocabulary Practice Exercise (Unit 47)

- **legacy** (n): something handed down from an ancestor or given in a will
- **deceased** (n): a person who has died
- **ardent** (adj): strong support or passionate about something
- **precocious** (adj): prematurely developed
- **precedent** (n): a previous or similar case serving as an example
- **intermediary** (n): a person acting as a go-between or mediator
- **truant** (n): a pupil who is absent from school without permission
- **visualize** (v): to form a mental picture of something or someone
- **volition** (n): your own will, action that is based on independent choice
- **ravenous** (adj): very hungry, greedy

Vocabulary Practice Test 47

1. Michael Jackson has left a ………………….. of great music to the world.
2. Mr. Roberts acted as an ………………… in the conflict between the girls and boys.
3. We heard that the ………………… passed away, leaving a fortune to me!
4. You need to ……………………..your success," said the boy's teacher, "It will motivate you."
5. The football fans showed their ……………………………….. support for their team during the World Cup final match.
6. Mark Farrel is proud that he joined the army on his own ………………….; without anyone's help.
7. The Judge said that there was no ……………………………..for this unique case.
8. The starving children ate their food …………………… then asked for more.
9. Due to her behaviour the …………………….. child is often mistaken for a teenager.
10. The boy's mum discovered that he had been a ………………….. for the whole week.

VERB FORMATION

Words	Verbs
imitation	
defence	
direction	
horror	
resident	
selection	
statement	

Vocabulary Practice Exercise (Unit 48)

- **incinerator** (n): something used to burn things in
- **disguise** (v): to hide, camouflage or cover up
- **ransack** (v): to search thoroughly, resulting in disorder
- **heritage** (n): inherited at birth, or deriving from tradition
- **enforce** (v): to compel obedience by threat
- **cutback** (n): a reduction in spending
- **curfew** (n): a fixed or imposed time to be indoors
- **daft** (adj): being silly, weak-minded
- **bereavement** (n): in a state of mourning the death of someone
- **berserk** (adj): going mad; being destructively violent or frenzied

Vocabulary Practice Test 48

1. It is essential that certain kinds of hospital wastes are disposed in ...., to avoid the spread of diseases.

2. Burglars .... the house, hoping they would find gold and jewellery.

3. The policeman was .... as an ordinary shopper, to catch thieves in the Supermarket.

4. The boy went .... when his I-phone was taken from him by a bully.

5. The prisoners are on a .... from 5pm to 6am each day.

6. "Don't be ....," said Daisy to her friend, "You can't jump over that bridge!"

7. The Prime Minister announced that there would be .... on spending in the country, over the next financial year.

8. Tom has difficulty dealing with the ....of his mum; he is continually sad and depressed.

9. There are many historic buildings that are categorised as English .... in England.

10. If you park on red lines in certain areas in London, the police will .... the law by towing your car away.

Challenge:
Where on the Cornish mainland would we find one of the world's most unusual botanical experiment; with more than 300 sub-tropical plants flowering in winter?

Vocabulary Practice Exercise (Unit 49)

- **intrude** (v): to go into someone's place without permission
- **nostalgia** (n): in a reflective frame of mind; looking back on fond memories
- **incurable** (adj): can't be cured, or made better
- **improvise** (v): to make up as you go along, without advance preparation
- **aftermath** (n): the result of something unpleasant e.g. storm or disaster
- **aggravate** (v): to worsen a situation; annoy or irritate
- **din** (n): a loud persistent noise
- **abode** (n): a home or dwelling
- **scarce** (adj): in very short supply
- **zealous** (adj): being full of excitement and enthusiasm

Vocabulary Practice Test 49

1. Dad installed an alarm so no one will ………………………… into our house.
2. Our parents often have ……………………… about their past memories.
3. I forgot my lines during my speech, so I had to……………………………………
4. Some diseases like cancer are ………………………………………
5. "Please don't ……………………… your brother, he's already upset," said mum.
6. Water is ………………… in some parts of Africa, especially when there is no rain.
7. "Please come into my humble ………………," she said cheekily to her friend.
8. Samantha is very ……………………… about taking part in our coming concert.
9. Amidst the ……………… outside there was screaming, loud talking and police sirens.
10. The couple stood outside their home in the ……………………………… of the hurricane and noticed that their roof had blown away.

SYNONYMS AND OPPOSITES

Words	Synonyms	Antonyms
sturdy		
allegation		
disclose		
transparent		
approval		
omission		
scorn		
valour		
deviate		
influential		

Crossword Puzzle No.13

Across

1. remembering fond memories
5. a system that selects its government
6. to spread widely or swallow up e.g. fire
7. consequence of an action
8. to void waste, spend wisely, use sparingly
10. to twist in pain

Down

2. to chase after someone and arrest them
3. cannot be defeated or destroyed
4. a person who has died
9. to force someone out of their position e.g. job

Vocabulary Practice Exercises (Unit 50)

- **unanimous** (adj): when everyone agrees with something
- **coherent** (adj): makes sense, logical, clear to understand
- **nominate** (v): to choose or select someone
- **philanthropist** (n): a person who performs charitable acts; loves mankind
- **authorize** (v): to give someone permission to do something
- **anonymous** (adj): showing no identity; having no name attached
- **sentimental** (adj): expressing tender emotions e.g. love
- **barricade** (v): to prevent access to people by locking them out
- **haphazard** (adj): random, not planned, by chance
- **artefact** (n): a product of human craftsmanship

Vocabulary Practice Test 50

1. My teacher .... me to look after the class in her absence.
2. Someone made an .... call to the Council to complain about noise.
3. The vote was ...., as everyone voted for me, so I won the competition.
4. Sally, the class monitor, was .... to be the School Councillor.
5. The gold chain and watch that my grandparents gave me are of .... value to me.
6. They erected the shed in a very .... way, that's why it fell during the strong winds last night.
7. Sir Richard Branson is a known .... who helps under-privileged children in developing countries.
8. The gunman ....himself inside the bank and refused to come out.
9. An archaeologist found some ....buried inside a mummy's tomb.
10. Most of the actors on stage were .... except one, who needed a mike.

VERB FORMATION

Words	Verbs
refurbishment	
contradiction	
conducive	
justification	
scrutiny	
oppression	
resolution	

Vocabulary Practice Exercise (Unit 51)

- **chiropodist** (n): a doctor who specializes in foot problems
- **chrysanthemum** (n): a colourful, autumnal English flower
- **posthumous** (adj): happening after someone's death
- **arrested** (v): to be taken by the police for doing wrong
- **exhume** (v): to have legal permission to dig up a dead body
- **obituary** (n): an announcement of a dead person, with details of his/her life
- **gullible** (adj): easily believes anything you're told
- **methodical** (adj): organized, orderly; something that is carefully done
- **distraught** (adj): to be frantic, full of anxiety and worry
- **allegiance** (n): showing loyalty to some group, a cause or to a country

Vocabulary Practice Test 51

1. They gave a .... award to the eminent scientist, a year after his death.
2. I gave mum a bouquet of .... for Mothers' Day.
3. The police .... the three men who burgled the house.
4. Investigators got permission to .... the body of a dead spy.
5. We heard about the Mayor's death from a newspaper ....
6. He went to see a .... because of problems with an in-growing toe nail.
7. The parents of the missing child were quite ...., before they found her.
8. On April Fool's Day, many people are .... when they are tricked.
9. The Scouts erected their tent in a very .... way, and won extra points for it.
10. Soldiers pledge .... to their country, when they join the army.

Words	Synonyms	Antonyms
imitate		
halt		
interior		
lament		
dusk		
assemble		
foe		
meager		
gruff		
loyal		

Vocabulary Practice Exercise (Unit 52)

- **colossal** (adj): huge, gigantic size
- **preoccupy** (v): to be completely absorbed in thought
- **grotesque** (adj): unnatural in shape, extremely ugly and bizzare
- **official** (adj): issuing something with authority
- **economise** (v): to avoid waste, spend wisely, use sparingly
- **abstain** (v): to hold yourself back from doing something
- **abstain** (n): neutral, not taking sides in voting
- **occupation** (n): what a person does for a job
- **loiter** (v): to hang around, wander about in an idle way
- **patriotic** (adj): showing strong support or love for your country

Vocabulary Practice Test 52

1. Although we heard rumours of an expected Royal baby, we had to wait for the ………………….. information.

2. Some people become extravagant when they are rich but nowadays many people try to ………………… on their spending.

3. The class took a vote during the debate, but five students chose to ……………………………… from voting.

4. "Please do not ………………………….. in the corridor," said the teacher, as she approached us.

5. For the Diamond Jubilee, they will erect a…………………………….. statute of the Queen in our local Shopping Centre.

6. I missed the question because I was ……………………………. with thoughts about my weekend birthday party.

7. Some horror films have ……………………….. characters which scare children.

8. During Ramadan, Muslim people ……………………………. from eating food during the daytime.

9. My dad's ……………………………, over the past 10 years, has been an Engineer.

10 At the international cricket match, many …………………………. people could be seen waving their own country's flags.

Did You Know? *Some words are always in the plural form? E.g. milk, scissors, trousers.*

Vocabulary Practice Exercise (53)

- **ingenious** (adj): clever, showing genius, very inventive
- **proprietor** (n): the owner of a business
- **veteran** (n): a person who has been a very long time in a job, or in the army
- **menial** (adj): lowly or sometimes degrading e.g. job
- **sedentary** (adj): requiring a great deal of sitting down e.g. type of job
- **manual** (adj): involving physical strength
- **flourish** (v): to be successful or famous; growing abundantly (e.g. plants)
- **amicable** (adj): friendly, peaceful, easy-going
- **entice** (v): to tempt or lure
- **forbid** (v): to command a person not to do something

Vocabulary Practice Test 53

1. We see many ………………….. in the Remembrance Day parade each year.
2. The farmer's crops will ……………..because he looks after his plants very well.
3. The Receptionist has a ……………….. job, so are those who work in offices.
4. "I would like to be a ……………………….. with my own staff," said the child.
5. Fishermen try to ………………… fish by putting worms on their fishing hooks.
6. The bank robbers thought that their plans were ……………………….. until they were caught!
7. Many workers provided…………………………labour when their machines broke down.
8. Despite doing a …………………..job, Mr. Brown goes on holiday each year.
9. The Theme Park rules ……………………….young children from going on some of the rides.
10. My neighbours are quite ………………people; we get on very well.

SYNONYMS AND OPPOSITES

Words	Synonyms	Antonyms
tranquil		
perish		
slender		
unison		
wealthy		
adjacent		
conceal		
escape		
feeble		
insolent		

Crossword Puzzle No.14

Across
1. huge, gigantic
4. unnatural in shape, extremely ugly
5. to give someone permission to do something
8. no identity, no name attached
9. something used to burn things in
10. strong or passionate about something

Down
2. legal or following the law
3. an incredible performance
6. managing the finances of a country
7. makes sense, logical, clear to understand

Vocabulary Practice Exercise (Unit 54)

- **tranquil** (adj): peaceful and quiet
- **vigilant** (adj): being alert or on the look out
- **boulders** (n): huge stones
- **restrict** (v): to limit someone's action, choice, movement
- **exterminate** (v): to get rid of something by destroy completely
- **obscene** (adj): indecent, repulsive, disgusting
- **scuffle** (v): to have a little rough fight
- **agile** (adj): very flexible, skillful
- **snare** (n): a trap that is set to catch something
- **apprentice** (n): someone who learns to do a job from an experienced Trainer

Vocabulary Practice Test 54

1. You must be .... when traveling at night on the underground.
2. Stonehenge is a tourist attraction, in Britain, with huge .... in a circle which fascinates everyone.
3. Our school library is a very ....place to study.
4. Two boys were sent to the Head teacher for hurting someone during a ....
5. The most ....gymnast was voted, "Winner of the Championship."
6. Two men were caught trying to lay a .... to catch elephants.
7. He was taken on as an ....to work with a firm of builders.
8. "We have to .... the opening times of the library," said the Librarian.
9. Children are warned not to watch .... things on their computers.
10. They called in experts to .... the mice in their basement.

Tick which words best describes you!

optimistic......	dependable.....	vivacious..........
indolent.........	bi-lingual........	contented..........
insolent.........	pessimistic......	pioneer............
garrulous......	discreet..........	innovative..........
diligent..........	influential.......	extravagant........
motivated......	eloquent..........	economic...........
uncouth........	placid.............	disdainful..........

Challenge: *This place which is 754 feed deep, holds more water than all the lakes in England, Scotland and Wales put together. If you're lucky you might see something there! It never freezes. Where is it?*

© 2018 Roselle Thompson   Vocabulary Skills for Practical Learning – Volume 1

Vocabulary Practice Exercise (Unit 55)

- **appetite** (n): feelings or desire you have for something e.g. food or power
- **inquisitive** (adj): being nosey; asking a lot of questions, prying
- **epilogue** (n): the concluding part of a play
- **enrich** (v): to make richer; add better value or greater significance
- **impudent** (adj): being bold with rudeness, brazen, saucy
- **deflated** (adj): feeling down; when a person's hopes are crushed
- **archaic** (adj): old, out of date and no longer in ordinary use (e.g. language)
- **smear** (v): to spread something on an object, e.g. butter on bread, smudge
- **vigorous** (adj): powerful action, strong; active or robust
- **quay** (n): a wharf, harbour

Vocabulary Practice Test 55

1. The .... boy was given detention by the Head teacher.
2. He felt .... because he was reprimanded in front of the whole class.
3. My neighbours are very ....; they want to know everything about me.
4. He has no ....for food due to the sad news he received.
5. We learnt about what happened to all the characters in the .... of the play.
6. Our school plans to .... our last week of term with lots of activities for the Diamond Jubilee.
7. Some words in English are now .... and sound rather strange in modern usage.
8. The Nursery Nurse washed the children who ....paint all over their faces.
9. Ten men unloaded the cargo from the boat which came into the ....
10. Athletes often have to do some .... exercises to warm up before their activities.

WORDS WHICH HAVE BEEN ABBREVIATED IN COMMON USAGE			
Auto	Automatic	**Mag**	magazine
Bus	omnibus	**Pram**	perambulator
Gym	gymnasium	**Piano**	pianoforte
phone	telephone	**Photo**	photograph
Cello	violoncello	**Prom**	promenade
Plane	aeroplane	**Exam**	examination

Challenge: *Which is the largest natural lake in England?*

Vocabulary Practice Exercise (Unit 56)

- **explicit** (adj): being precise; very clearly expressed
- **sinister** (adj): threatening or suggesting evil or harm
- **frantic** (adj): desperate, very anxious and worried
- **implement** (v): to put into practice (e.g. rule, law), carry out;
- **visionary** (n): a person with a keen foresight; who thinks of or plans ahead
- **sovereign** (n): a queen or king
- **demented** (adj): crazy, insane, mad
- **persecute** (v): to persist with harassing someone in order to make them suffer
- **exempt** (adj): free from a duty that others have to do but doesn't apply to you
- **heinous** (adj): horrific, evil, atrocious, abominable

Vocabulary Practice Test 56

1. Two students were .... from repeating Part One of the exams.
2. Although a new rule was agreed, it took a while to .... it in school.
3. The British .... celebrated her Diamond Jubilee in 2012.
4. Those who commit .... crimes are imprisoned for life.
5. An army leader needs to be a .... so that he can work out clever battle plans.
6. Dad became .... when he lost his car keys.
7. A 16 year old school girl was attacked by a .... man on a bus.
8. "Your directions were very ...., that's why I didn't get lost," he said.
9. My neighbours .... us, although we have tried to be friendly to them.
10. There is something dark and .... about the main character in that horror movie.

A Quick Test:
Give the meaning for the following words:

1. fugitive.............................
2. aroma...............................
3. condone............................
4. revoke..............................
5. longevity...........................
6. adjacent ....
7. avert..................................
8. intervene............................
9. peruse................................
10. recuperate..........................

Challenge: *Where would you find London's oldest jail?*

Vocabulary Practice Exercise (Unit 57)

- **disclaimer** (n): a document that refuses to accept responsibility for something
- **milliner** (n): a person who makes and sells hats only
- **hierarchy** (n): a system showing ranks of people, in order of importance
- **indifferent** (adj): not caring, not showing concern or interest
- **recollect** (v): to remember, to recall to mind, bring back to memory
- **passive** (adj): not actively involved in an activity, not taking part
- **interrogate** (v): to question formally or officially
- **incessant** (adj): continuous, with stopping
- **adamant** (adj): strict, without changing a decision made; unshakeable
- **atrocity** (adj): ruthless behaviour; horrible crimes against masses of people

Vocabulary Practice Test 57

1. The driver said that he could not .... what happened after the accident.
2. The police will ....a man they arrested, for stealing from a shop.
3. There is a .... in Britain's class structure.
4. Despite telling her about my loss, her attitude remained ....
5. It is very rare these days, to find a .... shop existing on its own; instead, they are sections within large department stores.
6. The library's ....notice refuses responsibility for all personal losses.
7. Children tend to talk .... and are often told to be quiet.
8. Sarah was very ....about not coming to my party.
9. We learnt about past leaders who have committed .... against people.
10. The children sat .... listening to their teacher, until a small boy spoke.

VERB FORMATION

Words	Verbs
digression	
stagnant	
application	
betrayal	
trickster	
location	
regression	
success	

Crossword Puzzle No.15

Across
4. happening after death
7. outdated, not in ordinary use e.g. language
8. a colourful autumnal English flower
9. to liven up, to strengthen

Down
1. to make richer, add better value
2. bold with rudeness, brazen, saucy
3. the owner of a business
5. a foot doctor
6. expressing tender emotions e.g. love
9. extremely clever, inventive

Vocabulary Practice Exercise (Unit 58)

- **fanatic** (adj): a person with extreme views, beyond normal limits
- **permissive** (adj): social behaviour that others might not approve of,
- **impervious** (adj): not penetrating; incapable of affecting, injuring or influencing
- **vocation** (n): a career, profession or job
- **suppress** (v): to hold back, keep within (e.g. feelings and emotions)
- **condolence** (n): the sympathy offered to someone who is experiencing sorrow
- **erratic** (adj): changeable, inconsistent or unpredictable behaviour
- **ignite** (v): to light up by making fire; to begin to burn
- **interactive** (adj): actively involved in; taking part in something
- **oriental** (adj): relating to the geographical area consisting of south eastern Asia

Vocabulary Practice Test 58

1. The vaults of the bank are supposed to be ……………………. to burglars.
2. We live in a …………………… society, where teenagers drink and take drugs.
3. Some religious …………………… believe that if they kill many people, they will be greatly rewarded when they die!
4. "Please accept my …………………… for your sad loss," she told her friend.
5. Some of the most successful restaurants are run by …………………… people from Hong Kong, Malaysia, China and Japan.
6. The child's behaviour has been quite …………………………. recently.
7. Jane finds it difficult to discuss her ………………….. feelings from childhood.
8. His ……………………., for the past ten years, has been in engineering.
9. Nowadays gas cookers don't need matches to …………………………. them.
10. The teacher's style of teaching is quite………………, so none of her pupils are passive.

LET'S LOOK BACK - YOU'RE ALMOST THERE!!

How do you think you've done so far? *Tick one of the boxes below:*

Excellent		Very Good		Good		Fair		Need more help	

Challenge: *What is Chatsworth House and what is it known for?*

Vocabulary Practice Exercise (Unit 59)

- **infantile** (adj): behaving like an infant, small child
- **prosperous** (adj): to be rich, wealthy
- **contradict** (v): to go against what someone says
- **mediate** (v): to bring about peace or agreement between parties
- **prejudice** (adj): unreasonable feelings or opinion about someone beforehand
- **rectify** (v): to repair or put right by correction, adjustment
- **repulsive** (adj): a feeling of disgust
- **melancholy** (adj): a gloomy or sad state of mind
- **encircle** (v): to surround something/someone
- **inflame** (adj): something that swells up e.g. part of the body

Vocabulary Practice Test 59

1. The main character in the novel is a man with ………… behaviour and speech.
2. Brothers and sisters often ……………………… each other and end up arguing.
3. My neighbour will need to ……………………… the damage done to my car.
4. Tom said that the Receptionist was ……………………… towards him.
5. An expert was sent to …………… between the two countries which are at war.
6. The pop star has become quite ……………, but extravagant with his money.
7. Some horror movies can be quite ………………… with lots of blood.
8. The woman looked ……………………… after hearing bad news.
9. Her joints are ……………………… and they are painful too, because she has arthritis.
10. The gang ……………………… the poor boy then they attacked him.

Write the **opposite** for these words

1. heroic ……………………………………
2. transparent ……………………………………
3. guilty ……………………………………
4. inferior ……………………………………
5. spendthrift ……………………………………
6. retreat ……………………………………

Challenge: *This City, 50 miles north of London, still has evidence of Viking and Bronze Age settlement, with a world class university founded in 1209 and ranked one of the top five universities in the world.*

Vocabulary Practice Exercise (Unit 60)

- **disfigure** (v): to ruin the appearance or beauty of someone or something
- **compatible** (adj): capable of working in different machines (e.g. computers)
- **poultry** (n): the meat of birds e.g. chicken, turkey, ducks, geese
- **hoax** (n): a trick, something intended to deceive or fool others
- **denigrate** (v): to speak damagingly about someone's character
- **diagnose** (v): to examine a person and say what's wrong with them
- **disarray** (adj): disorder or a messy state
- **contaminate** (v): to become impure by mixing with something bad or harmful e.g. bacteria or radioactive material
- **sufficient** (adj): enough, an adequate amount; plenty
- **rowdy** (adj): rough and disorderly; noisy disturbance

Vocabulary Practice Test 60

1. Most people eat more .... than red meat because it's cheaper.
2. It's important to buy software that is .... with your computer.
3. After her blood test, the doctor will .... what her sickness is.
4. The kidnappers attempted to .... their victims before torturing them.
5. They called off the bomb squad because the anonymous phone call was just a ....
6. The house was in .... after the burglars left.
7. People living in very poor countries are known to drink .... water.
8. Unfortunately, Maria does not have .... money for her travel ticket.
9. My sister and her friends were very ....during their sleepover party.
10. A popular program on TV at present is about bodies that are ....

Words	Synonyms
purchase	
prominent	
squander	
liberty	
deceased	
accomplice	

Challenge: *Which city is home to one of the largest New Year's celebrations in the world and famous for Hogmanay?*

Crossword Puzzle No.16

Across
2. bold and daring
4. horrific, evil, abominable
5. the concluding part of a play
6. behaving like an infant
9. expression of sympathy when someone dies
10. a document that refuses to accept responsibility

Down
1. feeling down and disappointed
3. to put into practice or start e.g. law
7. not able to penetrate
8. a system showing levels of importance

GLOSSARY – VOCABULARY WORD LIST

abode	apprentice	colossal
abstain	appropriate	commend
abstain	approve	commitment
absurd	archaic	committee
abundance	ardent	communal
abundant	aroma	commute
abyss	arrested	compatible
academic	arrogant	compel
accessible	artefact	comply
accommodation	ascent	composure
accomplish	aspire	concede
accumulate	assault	concise
accustomed	associate	condemn
acquaintance	atrocity	conditional
adamant	attire	condolence
adhere	audible	condone
adversity	authentic	conducive
affluent	authorize	congestion
aftermath	automation	consent
agenda	autonomous	console
aggravate	avert	conspire
aghast	banish	consult
agile	banter	consume
agitate	bedlam	contaminate
alight	bereavement	contemplate
allegation	berserk	contented
allegiance	betrayal	contract
alleviate	bi-annual	contradict
allocation	bi-lingual	contravene
altitude	binge	controversy
amiable	blemish	convenient
amicable	blunder	corpse
ample	boulders	cosmopolitan
amplify	breach	courteous
anecdote	broad	cravat
animated	cajole	cringe
animosity	calamity	culminate
annual	campaign	curfew
anonymous	candidate	curtail
antagonize	chaffing	customary
anxiety	chiropodist	cutback
apathy	chrysanthemum	cyclical
apparition	clemency	cynical
appease	coherent	daft
appetite	collaborate	dawdle
apprehend	collision	deceased

deceive	economise	fertile
decrepit	economy	fickle
define	efficacious	flamboyant
deflated	elect	flotsam & jetsam
delegate	eliminate	flounder
demented	eloquent	flourish
democracy	emancipate	foe
demolish	embark	forbid
denigrate	embezzle	foresight
denomination	eminent	formalize
depart	empower	formidable
depleted	emulate	fortitude
derelict	encircle	fractious
desist	endangered	fragment
despicable	endeavour	frailty
detain	enforce	frank
deterrent	engulf	frantic
deviate	enrich	frayed
diagnose	entice	frenzied
diagnose	epilogue	frock
digress	errand	fulfill
diligent	erratic	furore
diminutive	evade	furtive
din	evict	gallant
disarray	excavate	garner
disclaimer	excess	garrulous
disclose	exemplary	gaunt
discrete	exempt	generosity
disdain	exhume	gloat
disfigure	exodus	gorge
disguise	expedite	gratitude
dismal	explicit	gregarious
dismay	exterminate	grotesque
disparaging	extinguish	gullible
disperse	extol	haphazard
distended	extravagant	hazardous
distort	extrovert	hearty
distraught	fabricate	heckle
docile	facetious	heinous
domesticated	fanatic	heritage
drab	fatal	hierarchy
dubious	fatigue	hind
dupe	feasible	hinder
dynamic	feat	hindsight
eavesdrop	fellowship	hoax
eccentric	ferocious	humdrum

humiliate	insight	mobilize
hygienic	insipid	modern
hypocrite	insolent	monarch
ignite	installments	monumental
immense	instigate	morality
imminent	intensify	motivation
immobilize	intention	multitude
impart	interactive	nauseous
impeccable	intercept	nee
imperfections	intermediary	neglect
impervious	interrogate	negligence
implement	intersperse	nominate
impose	intoxicated	nostalgia
impoverish	introvert	notable
improvise	intrude	notify
impudent	intuition	notorious
inauguration	inundated	novice
incentive	invalid	nuisance
incessant	inventory	obituary
incinerator	invest	obscene
incision	invigorate	obsolete
incisive	irrational	obstinate
inclement	lavish	obstruct
incognito	legacy	obtain
incongruous	liberate	occupation
incurable	loathe	odour
indecision	locate	official
indelible	loiter	omen
indifferent	longevity	ominous
indolent	majority	omit
industrious	mammoth	opportunity
inevitable	manipulate	oppression
infantile	manual	optimistic
infatuated	manuscript	oriental
inferno	mar	orthodox
inflame	massive	oscillate
inflict	meager	ostracize
influence	mediate	oust
influential	melancholy	outburst
infuriate	menial	outlandish
ingenious	merchandise	outskirts
inherit	methodical	passive
initial	milliner	patriotic
injustice	misconstrue	penetrate
innovation	miser	penultimate
inquisitive	misgivings	peril

perish	rapid	scuffle
perks	rash	sect
permissive	ravenous	sedentary
persecute	recluse	seize
perspective	recollect	sentimental
peruse	recruit	serene
pessimistic	rectify	sever
Philantrophist	recuperate	sinister
phony	refrain	slumped
pioneer	refurbish	smear
placate	regiment	snare
placid	regress	sober
plausible	regulation	social
plummet	reimburse	solemn
pompous	reluctant	solidarity
portray	remedy	somber
posthumous	renowned	sorrow
potential	repercussion	sovereign
poultry	replenish	spouse
precarious	replica	spruce
precedent	reprimand	stagnant
precocious	repulsive	stale
predecessor	resemble	statistics
premeditated	reservation	steadfast
preoccupy	resident	stereotype
preside	resign	stimulation
pretentious	resolution	stingy
prior	restrain	stranded
prodigy	restrict	stray
prohibit	resuscitate	stringent
prolific	retain	submission
prominent	retire	substantial
prophesy	retrieve	suburbs
proprietor	revoke	succinct
prosecute	robust	sufficient
prospectus	rowdy	sullen
prosperous	rudimentary	summit
provisional	rural	suppress
provoke	sabotage	surmount
pulverize	sacrifice	swindle
purchase	saunter	symptoms
quaint	scarce	tangible
quay	scared	tattle
radiant	scent	tedious
ramification	scornful	temerity
ransack	scrutinize	tempestuous

tepid
territory
testimony
thrifty
tranquil
transient
transition
treacherous
trickster
truant
trudge
unanimous
uncanny
undisputed
unnerve
utilize
utilize
vacancy
valiant
vandalise
vehement
velocity
vendor
veneer
vengeance
versatile
veteran
vibrant
vice
vigilant
vigorous
violate
visionary
visualize
vocation
vociferous
volatile
volition
whimsical
wound
writhe
yield
zealous

ANSWERS TO TESTS

Vocabulary Test 1
1. approve
2. purchased
3. contented
4. remedy
5. incentive
6. miscarriage
7. liberate
8. allocate
9. placid
10. omitted

Vocabulary Test 2
1. eloquent
2. plummeted
3. excess
4. loathe
5. spouse
6. define
7. blunder
8. rash
9. flounder
10. curtailed

Vocabulary Test 3
1. consent
2. absurd
3. deceived
4. regulations
5. motivation
6. gloat
7. perished
8. scornful
9. bedlam
10. pompous

Vocabulary Test 4
1. indolent
2. diligent
3. refurbish
4. misgivings
5. refrain
6. deviate
7. drab
8. flamboyant
9. fickle
10. gregarious

Vocabulary Test 5
1. intention
2. replica
3. reservation
4. influential
5. resolution
6. oppression
7. conditional
8. yield
9. distorted
10. ostracized

Vocabulary Test 6
1. humiliated
2. portrayed

3. residents
4. renowned
5. thrifty
6. bi-lingual
7. restrain
8. aspiring
9. social
10. facetious

Vocabulary Test 7
1. discretely
2. optimistic
3. accustomed
4. resemble
5. provisional
6. pessimistic
7. stimulation
8. binges
9. notable
10. perspective

Vocabulary Test 8
1. installments
2. notorious
3. slumped
4. submission
5. outburst
6. derelict
7. impart
8. hinder
9. infuriate
10. aghast

Vocabulary Test 9
1. peruse
2. dismayed
3. gaunt
4. innovation
5. multitude
6. fatal
7. negligence
8. frayed
9. placate
10. gorged

Vocabulary Test 10
1. hypocrite
2. inclement
3. collaborate
4. digressed
5. allegation
6. initial
7. uncanny
8. appease
9. cynical
10. pulverise

Vocabulary Test 11
1. prospectus
2. fertile
3. stagnant

4. dynamic
5. surmount
6. decrepit
7. apparition
8. intercept
9. veneer
10. impoverished

Vocabulary Test 12
1. disclosed
2. utilizing
3. excavated
4. corpse
5. misconstrued
6. whimsical
7. obstinate
8. miser
9. agitate
10. retrieve

Vocabulary Test 13
1. invested
2. courteous
3. disparaging
4. perks
5. intensify
6. imminent
7. fabricated
8. marred
9. gallant
10. infatuated

Vocabulary Test 14
1. symptoms
2. outlandish
3. revoked
4. associates
5. penetrate
6. pretentious
7. invigorate
8. valiant
9. fatigued
10. vehement

Vocabulary Practice 15
1. condemned
2. consult
3. ferocious
4. ample
5. inherit
6. diagnosed
7. assaulted
8. banished
9. apathy
10. convenient

Vocabulary Test 16
1. robust
2. invalid
3. disperse

4. attire
5. dubious
6. foresight
7. conceded
8. calamity
9. comply
10. depleted

Vocabulary Test 17
1. velocity
2. manuscript
3. fellowship
4. omen
5. rural
6. hindsight
7. animosity
8. disdain
9. impose
10. tangible

Vocabulary Test 18
1. violating
2. prohibited
3. resuscitate
4. scrutinized
5. insight
6. outskirts
7. incognito
8. controversies
9. evade
10. accommodation

Vocabulary Practice 19
1. manipulate
2. unnerved
3. mobilized
4. sects
5. recuperate
6. abyss
7. automation
8. amiable
9. adversities
10. repercussion

Vocabulary Test 20
1. preside
2. apprehended
3. diminutive
4. cringed
5. formidable
6. reimburse
7. endeavour
8. fulfill
9. transition
10. commend

Vocabulary Test 21
1. condone
2. oscillates
3. animated

4. bantering
5. stringent
6. furore
7. Vice
8. transient
9. fractious
10. precarious

Vocabulary Test 22
1. intoxicated
2. insipid
3. succinctly
4. somber
5. dismal
6. volatile
7. duped
8. autonomous
9. antagonize
10. docile

Vocabulary Test 23
1. prominent
2. contravene
3. swindled
4. vandalise
5. intuition
6. penultimate
7. replenish
8. evicted
9. anecdote
10. writhed

Vocabulary Test 24
1. abundance
2. cajoled
3. accumulated
4. dawdled
5. frenzied
6. deterrent
7. tedious
8. vociferous
9. severed
10. chaffing

Vocabulary Test 25
1. utilize
2. delved
3. trudged
4. nuisance
5. inauguration
6. vengeance
7. plausible
8. ominous
9. rudimentary
10. treacherous

Vocabulary Test 26
1. fragments
2. affluent
3. peril

4. breach
5. distended
6. annual
7. morality
8. hygienic
9. anxiety
10. summit

Vocabulary Test 27
1. scared
2. massive
3. opportunity
4. compelled
5. extravagant
6. abundant
7. engulfed
8. rapidly
9. sorrow
10. sauntered

Vocabulary Test 28
1. errand
2. undisputed
3. console
4. testimony
5. extrovert
6. domesticated
7. culminated
8. merchandise
9. customary
10. phony

Vocabulary Test 29
1. solidarity
2. scent
3. novice
4. appropriate
5. incision
6. introvert
7. aroma
8. odour
9. emancipate
10. indecision

Vocabulary Test 30
1. wounded
2. arrogant
3. obstruct
4. stray
5. imperfections
6. prior
7. regiment
8. audible
9. notify
10. stranded

Vocabulary Test 31
1. depart
2. modern
3. impeccable

4. efficacious
5. indelible
6. blemishes
7. exemplary
8. broad
9. hind
10. steadfast

Vocabulary Test 32
1. recluse
2. compensate
3. garrulous
4. desist
5. serene
6. empowered
7. composure
8. amplify
9. alleviate
10. infamous

Vocabulary Test 33
1. extinguish
2. seized
3. reluctant
4. ascent
5. reprimanded
6. endangered
7. sullen
8. obtain
9. vendor
10. altitude

Vocabulary Test 34
1. longevity
2. contract
3. lavished
4. vibrant
5. cosmopolitan
6. extol
7. neglected
8. substantial
9. flotsam and jetsam
10. orthodox

Vocabulary Test 35
1. frocks
2. eminent
3. clemency
4. insolent
5. tempestuous
6. suburbs
7. stingy
8. bi-annual
9. sabotage
10. nauseous

Vocabulary Test 36
1. retire
2. detain
3. academic

4. cravats
5. quaint
6. locate
7. delegate
8. elect
9. resign
10. expedite

Vocabulary Test 37
1. adhere
2. accessible
3. denomination
4. embezzled
5. prosecute
6. trickster
7. inflicts
8. prolific
9. radiant
10. furtive

Vocabulary Test 38
1. generosity
2. garner
3. sacrificed
4. exodus
5. influence
6. inevitable
7. betrayal
8. prophesy
9. hazardous
10. majority

Vocabulary Test 39
1. monumental
2. irrational
3. conducive
4. cyclical
5. regress
6. sober
7. feasible
8. incisive
9. incongruous
10. frailty

Vocabulary Test 40
1. campaign
2. potential
3. commitment
4. vacancy
5. obsolete
6. despicable
7. acquaintances
8. demolish
9. conspired
10. stereotype

Vocabulary Test 41
1. provoked
2. industrious
3. collision

4. formalize
5. pioneers
6. recruit
7. solemn
8. accomplished
9. contemplating
10. premeditated

Vocabulary Test 42
1. inferno
2. fortitude
3. sprucing
4. stale
5. meager
6. commutes
7. frank
8. eavesdrop
9. humdrum
10. concise

Vocabulary Test 43
1. tattle
2. hearty
3. temerity
4. immobilized
5. statistics
6. heckled
7. inventory
8. inundated
9. predecessor
10. injustice

Vocabulary Test 44
1. instigate
2. agenda
3. emulate
4. authentic
5. interspersed
6. pampers
7. foe
8. nee
9. territory
10. committee

Vocabulary Test 45
1. candidate
2. economy
3. communal
4. democracy
5. monarch
6. consume
7. immense
8. prodigy
9. ramifications
10. eccentric

Vocabulary Test 46
1. tepid
2. mammoth
3. retain

4. feats
5. gratitude
6. alight
7. embark
8. congestion
9. eliminated
10. oust

Vocabulary Test 47
1. legacy
2. intermediary
3. deceased
4. visualize
5. ardent
6. volition
7. precedent
8. ravenously
9. precocious
10. truant

Vocabulary Test 48
1. incinerator
2. ransacked
3. disguised
4. berserk
5. curfew
6. daft
7. cutbacks
8. bereavement
9. heritage
10. enforce

Vocabulary Test 49
1. intrude
2. nostalgia
3. improvise
4. incurable
5. aggravate
6. scarce
7. abode
8. zealous
9. din
10. aftermath

Vocabulary Test 50
1. authorized
2. anonymous
3. unanimous
4. nominated
5. sentimental
6. haphazard
7. philanthropist
8. barricade
9. artefacts
10. coherent

Vocabulary Test 51
1. posthumous
2. chrysanthemum
3. arrested

4. exhume
5. obituary
6. chiropodist
7. distraught
8. gullible
9. allegiance
10. methodical

Vocabulary Test 52
1. official
2. economise
3. abstain
4. loiter
5. colossal
6. preoccupied
7. grotesque
8. abstain
9. occupation
10. patriotic

Vocabulary Test 53
1. veterans
2. flourish
3. sedentary
4. proprietor
5. entice
6. ingenious
7. manually
8. menial
9. forbid
10. amicable

Vocabulary Test 54
1. vigilant
2. boulders
3. tranquil
4. scuffle
5. agile
6. snare
7. apprentice
8. restrict
9. obscene
10. exterminate

Vocabulary Test 55
1. impudent
2. deflated
3. inquisitive
4. appetite
5. epilogue
6. enrich
7. archaic
8. smeared
9. quay
10. vigorous

Vocabulary Test 56
1. exempt
2. implement
3. sovereign
4. heinous
5. visionary
6. frantic
7. demented
8. explicit
9. persecute
10. sinister

Vocabulary Test 57
1. recollect
2. interrogate
3. hierarchy
4. indifferent
5. milliner
6. disclaimer
7. incessantly
8. adamant
9. atrocities
10. passively

Vocabulary Test 58
1. impervious
2. permissive
3. fanatics
4. condolence
5. oriental
6. erratic
7. suppressed
8. vocation
9. ignite
10. interactive

Vocabulary Test 59
1. infantile
2. contradict
3. rectify
4. prejudice
5. mediate
6. prosperous
7. repulsive
8. melancholy
9. inflamed
10. encircled

Vocabulary Test 60
1. poultry
2. compatible
3. diagnose
4. denigrate
5. hoax
6. disarray
7. contaminated
8. sufficient
9. rowdy
10. disfigure

ANSWERS to Quiz Challenges	Page
South Bank	3
The archipelago of St. Kilda, the remotest part of the British Isles	4
You can do so at shops which are London's Royal Warrant holders	5
The Victoria and Albert Museum	7
The British Museum	10
Hampton Court Palace	11
The History of World Museum	13
Entrance to the Royal residences and rare exhibits of a uniquely British blend of pageantry, tradition and history.	15
Hadrian's Wall	16
Stratford-upon-Avon	20
Houses of Parliament	23
Madam Tussaud	30
The National Gallery	31
The National History Museum	32
The London Eye	36
The Science Museum	37
York Minster	39
Tower of London	41

Royal Museums Greenwich	45
The Queen, Buckingham Palace	46
Kensington Palace	49
Royal Botanic Gardens, Kew, Richmond, London	50
Dorset England	54
Tower Bridge	55
The Royal Mews at Buckingham Palace is a working stable, and home to the royal collection of historic coaches and carriages, as well as the cars used for State occasions.	57
Stone Henge	60
Portmeirion, a hotel resort and a popular visitor attraction located on the coast of Snowdonia National Park in Gwynedd, North Wales.	64
The Norfolk Broads. It represents the mystic beauty of the rivers, with the fun and adventure that the whole family can enjoy.	66
Tresco Abbey Gardens	68
Loch Ness	76
Lake Windermere	77
Bankside	78
An exceptional country house in Derbyshire, home of the Duke & Duchess of Devonshire from 1549	81
Cambridge	82
Edinburgh	83

ANSWERS FOR VOCABULARY BUILDING EXERCISES

Page 6 – forming words with suffixes:

ed endings	*ed* endings	*able* endings	*ing* endings
• replied • prayed • delayed	• replied • prayed • delayed	• payable • justifiable • reliable	• buying • trying • obeying
ous endings	*er* endings	*ance* endings	*al* endings
• luxurious • furious • various	• heavier • dirtier • busier	• defiance • compliance • variance	• betrayal • denial • trial

Page 5

Put Prefixes in these words		**Put Suffixes in these words**	
fore/down/*broadcast*	fore/re/*tell*	exist/ence/ing/ed	remit/tance/ting/ted
multi/inter/*national*	in/*capable*	Simple/icity	creator/ion/ing
im/de/down/*press*	mis/*represent*	merciless/ful	postage/ing/
im/re/de/*port*	il/*logical*	momentous/ary/arily	human/ity
sub/*marine*	pre/*meditated*	interruption/ed/ive/or	cigar/ette
dis/un/*able*	mis/il/*treat*	comfortable/er/ing/ed	public/ation/ity/ly
un/re/*develop*	mis/pre/*judge*	eruption/ed	wait/er/ress/ing/ed

Page 6
VERB FORMATION

Nouns	Verbs
pleasure	please
knowledge	know
thought	think
choice	choose
laughter	laugh
injury	injure
loss	lose
remembrance	remember

Page 10
WORD-BUILDING
Adverbs: *loudly, peacefully, heavily, comfortably, sweetly, happily*

Page 13

Words	Synonyms (*similar*)	Antonyms (*opposites*)
approve	agree	disapprove
absurd	ridiculous	reasonable
liberate	free	caged
remedy	cure	poison
blunder	mistake	precise
plummet	fall	rise
loathe	hate	love

Page 14
NOUN FORMATION

Words	Nouns
liberate	liberation
omit	omission
content	contentment
approve	approval
eloquent	eloquence
define	definition
absurd	absurdity
deceive	deception

Page 15
NOUN FORMATION

Words	Nouns
compete	competition
humble	humility
permit	permission
hero	heroism
simple	simplicity
weigh	weight
sorry	sorrow
try	trial
vain	vanity
terrify	terror

Page 16
Form *Compound Words* – here are some suggestions. You may have formed others.

postbox	football	headache	snowman	outdoor	milkman	heartache
playground	flashlight	tablecloth	toothpaste	waterfall	shop	airplane
classroom	railway	cupboard				

Page 17
ADJECTIVE FORMATION

Words	Adjectives
fame	famous
fool	foolish
educate	educational
provision	provisional
custom	customary
magnet	magnetic
pure	purely
colony	colonial

Page 18
SYNONYMS AND OPPOSITES

Words	Synonyms (similar)	Antonyms (opposites)
garrulous	talkative	timid
regress	deteriorate	recover
vacant	empty	full
generosity	magnanimous	mean/stingy
pretend	false	genuine
dismay	surprise	pleasure
majority	most	few
vacate	leave	occupy
despicable	degrading	likeable
demolish	crush	construct

Page 20

Adjective	Verb	Noun
long	lengthen	length
wide	widen	width
instructional	instruct	instruction
residential	reside	residence
conclusive	conclude	conclusion
impressive	impress	impression

Page 24
SYNONYMS AND OPPOSITES

Words	Synonyms (similar)	Antonyms (opposite)
dispersal	scatter	gather
apprehend	catch	evade
recuperate	recover	worsen
stationary	still	mobile
courtesy	politeness	rudeness
seldom	rarely	frequently
contract	shorten	expand
sorrow	sadness	happiness
dwarf	short	tall
audible	distinct	unclear

Page 23
VERB FORMATION

Nouns	Verbs
adherence	adhere
accusation	accuse
recovery	recover
deception	deceive
receipt	receive
argument	argue
portrayal	portray
conversation	converse
permission	permit
exemption	exempt

Page 24
NOUN FORMATION - More Noun Formation to think about

Verbs	Nouns
invest	investment
consult	consultation
compel	compulsion
penetrate	penetration
revoke	revocation
banish	banishment
embrace	embrace
allocate	allocation
recruit	recruitment
depress	depression

Page 26
ADJECTIVES FORMATION

Nouns	Adjectives
ignorance	ignorant
wonder	wonderful
length	long
patience	patient
comfort	comfortable
fame	famous
beauty	beauty

Page 27
NOUN FORMATION

Verbs	Nouns
expel	expulsion
contravene	contravention
accumulate	accumulation
antagonise	antagonism
detain	detention
intrude	intrusion
intimidate	intimidation
rebel	rebellion
approve	approval
resemble	resemblance

Page 28
SYNONYMS AND OPPOSITES

Words	Synonyms (similar)	Antonyms (opposite)
mute	dumb	speak
inclement	dismal	bright
initial	first	last
peruse	examine	ignore
utilize	use	leave
abundance	many	scarce
respect	courteous	ill-mannered
reprimand	punishment	affection
concession	discount	extra/additional
thorough	careful	haphazard

Page 30

Add a **Suffix** to the following words:

fashion*able* sens*ible* expens*ive*

invita*tion* pain*ful* encourage*ment*

Page 31

Add a **Prefix** to the following words:
*il*legal *dis*respect *bi*annual *mis*trust *dis*able *un*willing
vice-captain *post*-war *bi*cycle *im*mortal *un*known *re*turn

Page 33
NOUN FORMATION

Words	Nouns
retaliate	retaliation
apprehend	apprehension
precise	precision
prominent	prominence
contravene	contravention
accumulate	accumulation
intrude	intrusion
forgive	forgiveness
affluent	affluence
extravagant	extravagance

Page 35
ADJECTIVE FORMATION

Words	Adjectives
distinct	distinctly
fury	furious
precision	precise
prominence	prominent
jubilee	jubilant
accumulation	accumulative
intruder	intrusive
detain	scornful
affluence	affluent
courage	courageous

© 2018 Roselle Thompson   Vocabulary Skills for Practical Learning – Volume 1

Page 42
NOUN FORMATION

Words	Nouns
expert	expertise
repatriate	repatriation
presume	presumption
intimidate	intimidation
censor	censorship
dejected	dejection
acquire	acquisition
empower	empowerment
proceed	procedure
intend	intention

Page 44
SYNONYMS AND OPPOSITES

Words	Synonyms (similar)	Antonyms (opposites)
permanent	indefinite	temporary
timid	shy	extrovert
concise	exact	longwinded
contest	dispute	agree
forbid	refuse	allow
solemn	serious	humorous
immense	colossal	diminutive
indolent	lazy	industrious
authorize	delegate	disallow

Page 46

Words	Synonym
insolent	rude
magnanimous	generous
hoax	trick
bereavement	sorrow
allegation	accusation

Page 48
VERB FORMATION

Nouns	Verbs
instigation	instigate
consumption	consume
receipt	receive
aspiration	aspire
presumption	presume
preoccupation	preoccupy
perseverance	persevere
deflation	deflate
recollection	recollect
permission	permit

Page 49
NOUN FORMATION

Words	Nouns
amend	amendment
distract	distraction
dedicate	dedication
delegate	delegation
generous	generosity
seize	seizure
ascend	ascent

Page 51
NOUN FORMATION

Words	Nouns
impudent	impudence
enrich	enrichment
diagnose	diagnosis
disfigure	disfigurement
adhere	adherence
compensate	compensation
interact	interaction

Page 53
SYNONYMS AND OPPOSITES

Words	Synonyms	Opposites
despise	hate	love
imminent	near	future
obsolete	old	modern
squander	waste	save
concise	exact	lengthy
outskirts	periphery	centre
diligent	industrious	indolent
publicise	broadcast	private
stubborn	obstinate	flexible
gloat	jeer	sympathise

Page 54
NOUN FORMATION

Words	Nouns
animated	animation
locate	location
retire	retirement
elect	election
resign	resignation
deviate	deviation
betray	betrayal
hazardous	hazard

Page 57
Adverb words:

1.	obediently	7.	abundantly
2.	impudently	8.	incredibly
3.	immediately	9.	painfully
4.	vigorously	10.	incessantly
5.	clumsily	11.	potentially
6.	seriously	12.	justifiably

Page 58
FORM VERB FROM THESE WORDS

Words	Verbs
recurrence	recur
suspension	suspend
enchantment	enchant
preoccupation	preoccupy
abstention	abstain
economy	economise
improvisation	improvise
perseverance	persevere
authorization	authorize
nomination	nominate

Page 59
SYNONYMS AND OPPOSITES

Words	Synonyms	Opposites
replenish	refill	deplete
condense	shorten	lengthen
motivate	encourage	discourage
notify	inform	withhold
obstruct	hinder	allow
depart	leave	exit
deceive	trick	honest
retain	keep	destroy
conspire	plot	reveal

Page 60
Give another word for the following:

1.	fatigue	tired	7.	Remedy	cure
2.	Obstinate	stubborn	8.	Sever	Cut off
3.	Wretched	unhappy	9.	Consume	eat
4.	Residence	home	10.	Statutory	legal
5.	Affectionate	loving	11.	Concise	precise
6.	Garrulous	talkative	12.	Solitude	loneliness

Page 62
SYNONYMS AND OPPOSITES

Words	Synonyms (similar)	Antonyms (opposite)
contemplate	consider	decisive
fabricate	lie	truth
accept	agree	refuse
abstain	avoid	accept
deliberate	intentional	accidental
occupation	job	unemployed
speculate	guess	precise
restrict	limit	unlimited
animated	lively	placid
presume	suppose	know

Page 63
VERB FORMATION

Words	Verbs
pretext	pretend
innovation	innovate
instigation	instigate
ignition	ignite
conspiracy	conspire
demolition	demolish
provocation	provoke
intervention	intervene
recruitment	recruit
resignation	resign

Page 67
VERB FORMATION

Words	Verbs
imitation	imitate
defence	defend
direction	direct
horror	horrify
resident	reside
selection	select
statement	state

Page 69
SYNONYMS AND OPPOSITES

Words	Synonyms (similar)	Antonyms (opposite)
sturdy	robust	weak
allegation	blame	truth
disclose	reveal	conceal
transparent	clear	opaque
approval	consent	disagreement
omission	oversight	remember
scorn	disdain	pride
valour	bravery	coward
deviate	divert	straight
influential	powerful	powerless

Page 71
VERB FORMATION

Words	Verbs
refurbishment	refurbish
contradiction	contradict
conducive	conduct
justification	justify
scrutiny	scrutinize
oppression	oppress
resolution	resolve

Page 72

Words	Synonyms (similar)	Antonyms (opposite)
imitate	copy	genuine
halt	stop	continue
interior	inside	exterior
lament	grieve	rejoice
dusk	twilight	dawn
assemble	gather	disperse
foe	enemy	friend/ally
meager	scanty	abundant
gruff	harsh	kind
loyal	true	treacherous

Page 74
SYNONYMS AND OPPOSITES

Words	Synonyms (similar)	Antonyms (opposite)
tranquil	peaceful	noisy
perish	destroy	build
slender	slim	obese
unison	togetherness	disharmony
wealthy	affluent	poor
adjacent	near	distant
conceal	hide	reveal
escape	elude	apprehend
feeble	weak	strong
insolent	rude	courteous

Page 78
A Quick Test:
Give the meaning for the following words:

1.	fugitive	an escaped prisoner	6.	adjacent	near
2.	aroma	smell of good	7.	avert	avoid
3.	condone	encourage to do bad	8.	intervene	get involved
4.	revoke	take back what's given	9.	peruse	check carefully
5.	longevity	long life	10.	recuperate	recover

Page 79
VERB FORMATION

Words	Verbs
digression	digress
stagnant	stagnate
application	apply
betrayal	betray
trickster	trick
location	locate
regression	regress
success	succeed

Page 82
Write the **opposite** for these words:

1.	heroic	coward
2.	transparent	opaque
3.	guilty	innocent
4.	inferior	superior
5.	spendthrift	squander
6.	retreat	advance

Page 83

Words	Synonyms
purchase	buy
prominent	noticeable
squander	waste
liberty	freedom
deceased	dead
accomplice	Partner/ally

ANSWERS FOR CROSSWORD PUZZLES

Crossword Puzzle No. 1

ACROSS	DOWN
4 omit	1 purchase
5 liberate	2 eloquent
7 placid	3 motivate
9 contented	6 blunder
	8 remedy
	9 consent

Crossword Puzzle No. 2

ACROSS	DOWN
3 absurd	1 gloat
5 indolent	2 consent
7 diligent	4 misgivings
9 regulations	6 deviate
10 refurbish	8 drab

Crossword Puzzle No. 3

ACROSS	DOWN
3 replica	1 aspire
4 optimistic	2 humiliate
7 resemble	5 influential
9 reservation	6 social
10 conditional	8 taunt

Crossword Puzzle No. 4

ACROSS	DOWN
1 digress	2 innovation
3 uncanny	4 neglect
6 allegation	5 recruit
7 notorious	8 peruse
8 placate	
9 slump	

Crossword Puzzle No. 5

ACROSS	DOWN
5 excavate	1 cohabit
6 stagnant	2 penetrate
7 fabricate	3 invest
10 perks	4 reprimand
	8 revoke
	9 compel

Crossword Puzzle No. 6

ACROSS	DOWN
3 consult	1 dubious
4 attire	2 solitude
6 institute	5 corpse
8 embrace	6 imposter
9 rectify	7 tranquil

Crossword Puzzle No. 7

ACROSS	DOWN
5 velocity	1 violate
6 hoard	2 retaliate
7 disdain	3 prohibit
8 scrutinise	4 repercussion
9 meticulous	
10 diagnose	

Crossword Puzzle No. 8

ACROSS	DOWN
4 animated	1 intoxicated
5 dismal	2 condone
6 apprentice	3 conducive
10 premeditated	7 regal
	8 dupe
	9 amass

Crossword Puzzle No. 9

ACROSS	DOWN
4 aroma	1 imminent
6 novice	2 inclement
7 extravagant	3 prominent
8 affluent	5 merchandise
10 indolent	9 minute

Crossword Puzzle No. 10

ACROSS	DOWN
3 garrulous	1 odour
5 fugitive	2 justify
7 longevity	4 recuperate
9 alleviate	6 conspire
10 deceive	8 notify

Crossword Puzzle No. 11

ACROSS	DOWN
3 adhere	1 embezzle
5 demolish	2 provoke
6 hazardous	3 acquaintance
7 pessimistic	4 industrious
9 obsolete	8 insolent

Crossword Puzzle No. 12

ACROSS	DOWN
1 monarch	2 consume
4 agenda	3 formalise
7 immobilise	5 accomplish
8 contemplate	6 intervene
9 instigate	8 concise

Crossword Puzzle No. 13

ACROSS	DOWN
1 nostalgia	2 apprehend
5 democracy	3 invincible
6 engulf	4 deceased
7 repercussion	9 oust
8 economy	
10 writhe	

Crossword Puzzle No. 1 4

ACROSS	DOWN
1 colossal	2 legitimate
4 grotesque	3 feat
5 authorise	6 economy
8 anonymous	7 coherent
9 incinerator	
10 ardent	

Crossword Puzzle No. 15

ACROSS	DOWN
4 posthumous	1 enrich
7 archaic	2 impudent
8 invigorate	3 proprietor
9 invigorate	5 chiropodist
	6 sentimental
	9 ingenious

Crossword Puzzle No. 16

ACROSS	DOWN
2 audacious	1 deflated
4 heinous	3 implement
5 epilogue	7 impervious
6 infantile	8 hierarchy
9 condolence	
10 disclaimer	

Certificate of Achievement

This *Phoenix Certificate* is presented to

....

For successfully completing

Vocabulary Skills for Students & Teachers: – A Practical Learning Tool Kit Volume 1

Score Achieved ☐

Comment...
....

Teacher/Parent Signature...

© 2018 Roselle Thompson   Vocabulary Skills for Practical Learning – Volume 1

About the Author

Roselle Thompson B.A Hons, MPhil, has over 27 years of experience in teaching and education development in the UK. In addition to writing, Roselle has been creating since 1994, intensive courses in a number of subjects; including English (language and literature), Maths, Science, Verbal Reasoning and Public Speaking for children from as young as 5 years old, to GCSE and 6th Form A level English Language and Literature. Roselle also organises extra support Tutorials for undergraduates struggling in their first year at university. Roselle is a Poet, Broadcaster and International Speaker; and her approach is therefore to make her significantly accumulated skills available to her students for their personal empowerment, development and life-long success.

BOOKS IN THE SERIES BY THE SAME AUTHOR...............

ENGLISH GRAMMAR: A STUDENT'S COMPANION

This book prepares children for the 11+ independent and state grammar schools as well as the Key Stage 2 SATs tests. Although there are a variety of grammar books on the market, this book is based on over 27 years of the Author's techniques based on teaching and heading schools and rigorously tested exercises done in both school and tuition classrooms. The book contains a thorough preparation in grammar and valuable exercises for all aspects of foundation English literacy development up to the age of 13 years.

MASTERING COMPREHENSION SKILLS

This book provides a complete package of introduction, revision and practice comprehension passages to help you with preparation for the Key Stage 2 SATs tests and those preparing for the 11+ independent and state grammar school tests. The format of the questions replicates the SATs Reading and Comprehension tests to help your child become familiar with the format of the tests.

SPELLING & WORD POWER SKILLS

This structured spelling course was written to develop essential spelling skills for both individual use and group work in the classroom. It will help you to learn spelling techniques to improve your vocabulary knowledge and develop your word-power skills. It is designed to encourage you to read and understand how words are formed, their relationship with each other, followed by practical spelling activities.

VOCABULARY SKILLS FOR PRACTICAL LEARNING

The Vocabulary book contains over 60 Units & 60 Unit Tests, which can be used as lessons, with a total of 600 vocabulary words. Each Unit presents at least 10 vocabulary words which show their class or part of speech, together with their definition. This is followed by 60 gap-filling worksheet exercises for you to complete, without looking at the meaning.

Each gap-filling exercise helps students to see how these words are used in their contexts and tests the child's knowledge of them. You should learn these lists of words with their meaning for each unit before you take the test. There are also 16 crossword puzzles which are designed to help you consolidate your learning and also for you to enjoy and have fun while expanding your vocabulary.

Learning vocabulary should not be a mechanical or robotic experience but one in which children come alive when they discover that their knowledge is a form of power which gives them mastery of the English language when they use them. Check out 39 general knowledge Challenges set throughout the book, as well as interesting brain teasing crossword puzzles!

Teachers will find this book useful as the exercises here can either be used in group work or for individual learners to use at their own pace in the classroom and for extended work at home. This book therefore has a dual purpose – it not only teaches and expands but tests students' overall mastery of their vocabulary as they develop. Also included in this book is your reward, a Certificate of Achievement, which marks our successful completion of this book. A glossary of all the words used in this book is listed alphabetically, with an answer key for the worksheets at the back of the book.

> *Do You Know?* With hard work, you can achieve whatever you aim for? Good luck! We will see you again in the next book – **Building Vocabulary Skills for Success - Book 2.**

www.ingramcontent.com/pod-product-compliance
Lightning Source LLC
Chambersburg PA
CBHW080833010526
44112CB00015B/2503